Preface 前言

This book consists of almost all the idioms and expressions collected from College Board practice tests and real tests that are most frequently used and asked in SAT, ACT, and GMAT.

When I help students with SAT and ACT, there are an numerous number of books about words and grammar with different approaching styles, which students easily look up and refer to. However, even though idioms and expressions take up over 30 percent of the sentence structures and writing questions in SAT and ACT, there was no book about them for students to get help from.

This book is structured for students to learn idioms and expressions in SAT and ACT writing question styles. After introducing definitions of each idiom and expression, this book provides practice questions for those idioms and expressions. After familiarizing with idioms and expressions, students can test their ability to handle those idioms and expressions with the real test questions close to the actual writing questions in SAT and ACT, and the idioms and expressions should help understand and use in GMAT and GRE reading and writing.

This one book is enough for students to learn idioms and expressions and master the usage of them. Also teachers and instructors can have more practice tests they can use during the classes.

With a very short period of studying this book, I wish students can find the missing part for their perfect score.

本书的内容包括来源于 SAT、ACT 和 GMAT 的官方指南及真题中出现的几乎所有短语。

在多年的 SAT 和 ACT 教学过程中，笔者曾遇到过许许多多不同风格单词和语法书，考生基本上都能够很容易找到并将其作为参考。但是，尽管短语几乎占句子结构和写作问题的 30%，我们却仍然找不到任何一本仅关于此范畴的可供参考和使用的书籍。

笔者编写本书的主要目的是帮助考生系统地学习在 SAT、ACT 写作问题中频繁出现的短语。在详细介绍每一个短语的意思之后，本书还提供了练习题供考生练习如何使用短语。在熟悉了这些短语之后，考生可以使用本书提供的基本上等同于 SAT 和 ACT 真题水平的练习题去测试自己对于这些短语的掌握程度，另外掌握这些短语同样可以帮助考生提高考试中的写作水平。

本书对于 GMAT 和 GRE 考试中短语的覆盖程度极大，考生完全可以通过对本书的学习进而掌握考试中的短语。本书也为授课教师提供了课堂教学中可以使用的极好的教学素材。

笔者希望考生可以通过对这本书短时间的学习，能够完善自己的知识进而争取得到更好的成绩。

本书的译者为李光祎，在本书的编写过程中还得到以下几位老师的帮助，他们分别是：李鑫、靳丹梦、孙洪雨、王鑫、陈蕾、吕小雯、蒲雯和刘玲。

洪龙杓

2015 年 5 月

thebeyond2005@hotmail.com

SAT&ACT 短语及逗号用法，只要一本就掌握

The Only Book for Idioms,Expressions,and Commas for SAT&ACT

【韩】洪龙杓 / 主编

大连理工大学出版社
Dalian University of Technology Press

图书在版编目(CIP)数据

SAT&ACT短语及逗号用法，只要一本就掌握 /（韩）洪龙杓主编. — 大连 : 大连理工大学出版社，2015.6

ISBN 978-7-5611-8931-3

Ⅰ.①S… Ⅱ.①洪… Ⅲ.①英语—语法—高等学校—入学考试—美国—自学参考资料 Ⅳ.①H314

中国版本图书馆CIP数据核字(2015)第123535号

大连理工大学出版社出版

地址:大连市软件园路80号　邮政编码:116023

发行:0411-84708842　邮购:0411-84703636　传真:0411-84701466

E-mail:dutp@dutp.cn　　URL:http://www.dutp.cn

大连住友彩色印刷有限公司印刷　　大连理工大学出版社发行

幅面尺寸:185mm×260mm　　印张:10　　字数:160千字

印数:1~4000

2015年6月第1版　　2015年6月第1次印刷

责任编辑:马嘉聪　　责任校对:金强

封面设计:王付青

ISBN 978-7-5611-8931-3　　定　价:28.00元

How to use this book

如何使用本书

When 'be' is put at the beginning, the idioms and expressions are mostly about Adjectives, but if the idioms and expressions do not have 'be' in the beginning, they are about Verbs and Nouns.

Ex) be good at / consist of

Each unit has definitions, grammar explanations, and practice questions about related idioms and expressions. I made 20 practice questions first and listed up idioms and expressions later that the number of idioms and expressions in each unit can be different.

When going through each practice question, students should write down their own answer in the "Correction" part.

Ex) Correction: replace 'to' with 'in'

I put together idioms and expressions alphabetically at the end of the book for students to locate conveniently, and also mixed 20~ 30 idioms and expressions in each unit to prevent boredom by having a set of mixed up idioms and expressions to study every day.

In the practice test in each unit will only ask about the idioms and expressions for the unit, but in the real tests, the questions are not only about idioms and expressions. Students will practice the questions in the real tests close to the actual SAT and ACT questions.

By repeating practice of practice questions and real tests, students will easily comprehend the idioms and expressions.

This book does not have many high level words because the main focus is to study idioms and expression.

Grammar explanations are only for relative idioms and expressions. Detailed grammar will be dealt in the sequential books. Pretest is the same level as the real tests, and also students can check their procedure following DAY schedule.

1. 当书中的短语前有“be”的时候，该词组为形容词。但是，如果没有 “be” 在词组前，那么该词组为关于动词或者名词的词组。

例如： be good at / consist of

2. 书中的每一个单元都将有定义、语法解释和练习题部分。笔者先提供了 20 道练习题，然后列举了短语，不过每一个单元的短语数量可能会有所不同。

在做每一道练习的时候，建议大家在“Correction”部分写下自己的答案。

例如： Correction: replace ‘to’ with ‘in’

3. 书后短语汇总表按首字母顺序进行排列，以便于查找。书中每个单元包含 20~30 个短语的列表，采用乱序排列，以有效地避免每天学习和记忆中的枯燥乏味。

4. 只有本单元所提及的短语才会出现在该单元的练习题当中，但是，书后的测试题所覆盖的范围则不仅仅包括短语，大家将会体验到接近于 SAT 和 ACT 真题难度的测试题。

5. 通过单元后练习题和书后的综合测试题，大家会更深入地理解书中的短语。

6. 本书所使用的词汇相对简单，主要用意在于使学生更多地关注短语的用法。

7. 语法解释仅仅会在一些特殊或重要的短语处出现。更加详细的语法解释会在本书的续篇中陈述。书前的摸底测试难度接近真题水平。另外，大家可以利用书中的时间表安排学习时间。

目录

Contents

PRETEST

1. Students, who excel in (A) sports, should not limit themselves to (B) physical development; in order to succeed in (C) the professional sports world, they need to be also well (D) at academic subjects. No error (E)

2. Cell phones these days have been (A) equipped with (B) almost all the advanced functions (C), which traditional computers were used to (D) have. No error (E)

3. Filling out (A) the investigation forms with stock-in-trade (B) stories that could happen in every operation, Dan was now afraid that his partner Sid would not cooperate with (C) the story (D). No error (E)

4. Rachel felt like wearing (A) the high heels for a change (B) this morning, being fired (C) from the job (D) last week. No error (E)

5. Though Ray was very nice when (A) he was with the rest of the platoon, as a trainer for snipers (B), he did not give (C) any face, with which (D) he was acquainted, any break during the training session. No error (E)

6. Sami's dog always runs away (A) with the sight of (B) a cat, a weird behavior (C) unique to (D) her dog. No error (E)

7. The emergency room was filled with (A) doctors wanting (B) to see the rare patient, that (C) had the green mole on the shoulder (D). No error (E)

8. James, who has never participated in (A) any official race, goes to school on foot (B) every day in an effort of training (C) himself for a track race (D). No error (E)

9. The countries which quickly emerged from (A) feudalism was (B) industrialized before (C) other countries nearby, gaining an edge over (D) them. No error (E)

10. Money was raised by the hospital administrators, enabling Kenneth to receive (A) a heart transplant operation; this (B) reminded many people in the hospital, such as doctors, nurses,

and patients, with the movie *John Q*, which resembled Kenneth's situation. No error
C D E

11. Unlike what many believe, the kiwi fruit is native in China, but named after the kiwi bird in New Zealand; most of the kiwi fruit consumed in the world is produced in New Zealand, so it was commercially beneficial for New Zealand to call it Kiwi when it started to be produced in New Zealand. No error
A: native in China B: named after the kiwi bird C: New Zealand; most D: commercially beneficial E: No error

12. Last spring the South Korean government combined with three official bodies regarding disaster and rescue in response to the dropping support rate for the government. No error
A: Last spring B: combined with C: regarding D: in response to E: No error

13. When Ms. Michelle wanted to confirm if John would come to participate to the presentation the next day, he was hesitating to give an answer, so she could know he was inconsistent with his earlier statement in the presence of his parents. No error
A: if John would come B: participate to C: inconsistent with D: in the presence of E: No error

14. Although Dillon went to India in search of opportunity, he had never expected to meet and get married with an Indian woman, who would enable him to succeed internationally. No error
A: Although B: in search of C: had never expected D: with E: No error

15. When Rosie moved to the city, she had to adjust to many cases; she neither knew how to take a cab or understood how to use the subway. No error
A: When B: adjust to C: or D: understood E: No error

16. On entering the exhibition, the painting made sense to me because it was rarely distinct from other paintings of the artist. No error
A: the painting made sense to me B: it C: rarely D: distinct from E: No error

17. Some of Korean soap operas' appeal to an astronomical number of viewers in Asia is comparable to or bigger than Hollywood stars in the same region. No error
A: to B: astronomical C: to D: Hollywood stars E: No error

18. In recognition of James' extraordinary ability of writing songs, Cindy called his manager, wishing to collaborate with James. No error
A: In recognition of B: of writing C: wishing D: collaborate with E: No error

19. Mr. Jonathan did not like to fix Lucy's essays as deep as other students' on account of her pride. No error
A: as deep as B: other students' C: on account of D: pride E: No error

20. Most of the residents in the island are convinced of the significance of the policy ralating with the fish quota. No error
A: are B: of C: ralating with D: fish quota E: No error

21. On the brink of (A) an explosive altercation between Han and Linda, George, a Chemistry teacher, (B) who was inadvertently passing by, (C) entering (D) the classroom. No error (E)

22. Jerry wanted to quit the current job and leave the city as much as (A) he had come to terms with (B) the job, which made him helplessly, (C) and the city, where his ex-wife was living. (D) No error (E)

23. After coming down of a cold (A) frequently during (B) the winter, Jeffrey endowed the vice president Helen with (C) the full authority of the clothing line and spent more time playing (D) golf. No error (E)

24. Johnson stopped by (A) Jane's apartment and saw Henry's bag in the study by accident, (B) but did not ask if she invited Johnson by design (C) to show there was something going on between she (D) and Henry. No error (E)

25. Prior to (A) the Modernism, art organizations were mainly made up of (B) painters who did their best to (C) draw the objects as real as cameras. (D) No error (E)

26. With his clumsy art in display (A) in his office, the chairman Suri also adheres to (B) the works of art (C) by the unknown artists from the third world (D) such as North Korea. No error (E)

27. The local government do not encourage expatriates to respond to (A) unfair and unjust (B) scenes among the local people; in fact, (C) they are discouraged to engage (D) in any kind of dispute with the local people. No error (E)

28. Doctors these days (A) do not tell patients seriously (B) about their symptoms having (C) confidence about (D) their skills. No error (E)

29. Martha receives (A) many feelers about her interest in working (B) for news agencies since her publication about (C) journalism's impact on (D) economy last year. No error (E)

30. Not wanting (A) to skip the assigned amount of water intake, 28 ounces of water was consumed by Betty (B) before sleep last night according to (C) the daily diet regimen. (D) No error (E)

ANSWERS

1. D 把 well 改成 good

Idiom in use excel in (在……方面出色)，limit ~ to (把……限制在)，succeed in (在……中获得成功)，be good at (擅长)

2. D 去掉 were

be used to 意为习惯于，而在这里根据句子的本意应使用 used to，意为“曾经……”。

Idiom in use be equipped with (装备)，be used to...ing (习惯于……)，used to (曾经……)

3. D 把 story 改成 stories

在本句当中，story 指第一行中的 stories，所以改成 stories。

Idiom in use fill out (填 写)，stock-in-trade (存 货)，be afraid of (害 怕)，cooperate with (与……合作)

4 C 把 being 改成 having been

本句需要考虑主从复合句的时态对比问题，应使用现在完成时的分词形式。

Idiom in use feel like...ing (想要)

5. E

Idiom in use be acquainted with (熟悉)，give a break (休息一下)

6. B 把 with 改成 at

Idiom in use at the sight of (看见……时)，be unique to (对……唯一，独特)

7 C 把 that 改成 who

that 不能用在逗号后，这里替换成 who 引导修饰人的非限定性定语从句。

Idiom in use be filled with (充满着……)

8 C 把 of training 修改成 to train

Idiom in use participate in (参与)，on foot (步行)，in an effort to (企图)

9. B 把 was 改成 were

由于主语是 countries，所以 be 动词应该使用 were。

Idiom in use emerge from (从……中出现)，gain an edge over (获得优势)

10 C 把 with 改成 of

Idiom in use enable A to B (使 A 能够 B)，remind A of B (提醒 A 关于 B)

11. A 把 in 改成 to

Idiom in use native to (原产于)，name after (以……命名)

12. B 去掉 with

Idiom in use in response to (对于……做出反应)

13. B 把 to 改成 in

Idiom in use participate in (参 与)，consistent with (与 …… 一 致)，in the presence of (在……面前)

14. D 把 with 改成 to

Idiom in use in search of (寻找)，get married to (与……结婚)，enable A to B (使 A 能够 B)

15 C 把 or 改成 nor

Idiom in use adjust to (调整，调节)，neither A nor B (既不是 A 也不是 B)

16. A 把 the painting made sense to me 改成 I made sense of the painting

在本句当中，on entering 的主语是一个人（主动语态），而不是画，所以做如上修改。

Idiom in use make sense of (搞清……的意思)，be distinct from (不同于)

17. D 在 Hollywood stars 前面加上 that of

当作比较的时候，需要把比较双方陈述清晰，在本句中，与 Korean soap opera's appeal 相比的是 the appeal of Hollywood stars。

Idiom in use a number of (许多)，be comparable to(with) (与……可比较)

18. B 把 of writing 改成 to write

Idiom in use in recognition of (为酬答……而)，have an ability to (有能力做)，collaborate with (与……合作)

19. A 把 deep 改成 deeply

在句中修饰动词 fix，需要改成副词形式。

Idiom in use on account of (由于)

20 C 把 with 改成 to

Idiom in use be convinced of (确信)，relating to (涉及，与……有关系)

21. D 把 entering 改成 entered

原句缺少动词作为谓语成分，因此改为 entered。

Idiom in use on the brink of (濒于)，pass by (经过)

22 C 把 helplessly 改成 helpless

helplessly 在这里用来修饰 him，因此需要使用形容词形式。

Idiom in use come to terms with （与……达成协议)

23. A 把 of 改成 with

Idiom in use come down with (染上 , 得了……病)，endow A with B (把 A 捐赠给 B)

24. D 把 she 改成 her

Idiom in use stop by (顺便拜访)，by accident (偶然地)，by design (故意地)，between A and B (在 A 和 B 之间)

25. D 在 cameras 后加上 could take

本句的比较不清晰，the object as real as cameras 这部分表达不清晰，需要补足谓语动词以明示。

Idiom in use prior to （在……之前)，be made up of （由……组成)，do one's best to (尽力做……)

26. A 把 in 改成 on

Idiom in use on display (展出)，adhere to (遵循)

27. D 把 to engage 改成 from engaging

Idiom in use respond to (对……做出回应)，encourage A to B (鼓励 A 做 B)，discourage A from B (阻止 A 做 B)，engage in (参加，从事)

28 C 在 having 前加逗号

having 在这里用来修饰 symptoms，但是根据句子的意图，这里 having 的逻辑主语应该是 the doctors，因此做如上修改。

29. A 把 receives 改成 has received

在用 since 引导的时间状语的情况下，应使用现在完成时。

Idiom in use interest in (对……的兴趣)，impact on (影响)

30. B 把 28 ounces of water was consumed by Betty 改成 Betty consumed 28 ounces of water

本句以 Not wanting 开头（主动语态），暗指主语是一个人，因此做如上修改。

Idiom in use an amount of (许多)，according to (根据，按照)

UNIT 1

DAY 1

PART 1 BRIEF GRAMMAR FOR IDIOMS AND EXPRESSIONS

PART 2 PRACTICE QUESTIONS

PART 3 ANSWERS

DAY 1

PART 1 BRIEF GRAMMAR FOR IDIOMS & EXPRESSIONS

动词不定式和动名词

1. 最常与动名词连用的动词如下：

avoid, admit, complete, consider, deny, enjoy, escape, evade, feel like, finish, keep, mind, miss, postpone, practice, quit, resist, reject, suggest, and so on.

这些动词后面需接动名词

Ex) She did not mind turning on the air conditioner even though she was having a mild cold. (在这种情况下，“mind to turn”属于错误的用法)

2. 最常与动词不定式连用的动词如下：

decide, desire, expect, hope, need, learn, manage, promise, refuse, want, wish, and so on.

Ex) Lisa decided to take another course. (这些动词后面需接动词不定式)

3. 既可以与动词不定式搭配也可以与动名词搭配的动词如下：

begin, be worthwhile, cease, continue, hate, like, love, prefer, propose, start, and so on.

Ex) Sam continued to watch the movie.(正确)

Ex) Sam continued watching the movie.(正确)

4. 以下词汇 demand, require, recommend, decide, insist, suggest, propose, order, command, necessary, essential, important, desirable, decision, suggestion, wish 均可表达强迫或者义务的意思，后接从句应使用虚拟语气，也就是说当他们与 that 连用的时候从句动词应使用 should+ 动词原形，或者在很多情况下省略 should，直接使用动词原形。

Ex) Nina suggested that the taxi driver should drive faster. (正确)

Ex) Nina suggested that the taxi driver drive faster. (正确)

Ex) Nina suggested that the taxi driver drove faster. (错误)

Ex) Nina suggested that the taxi driver drives faster. (错误)

PART 2 PRACTICE QUESTIONS

Choose an incorrect answer and write the correct form in the *Correction.*

1. Harry wanted to (A) reject to participate (B) in the talent show, but his sister insisted by saying that she would (C) be happy to see (D) him perform.

✓ *Correction:*

2. The movie was worth to watch (A); plots, characters, and (B) visual and sound (C) effects were all above (D) my expectation.

✓ *Correction:*

3. Kevin finally finished to sing (A) after trying (B) more than two hours, making (C) the whole cameramen exhausted (D).

✓ *Correction:*

4. Lou got furious at (A) the news that Sunny, second in command, (B) had postponed to visit (C) the car factory without telling (D) him anything.

✓ *Correction:*

5. Although (A) Jim needed to have (B) his computer fixed (C), he kept to use (D) it until he made enough money to buy a new one.

✓ *Correction:*

6. Lisa hates watching (A) horror movies because she cannot escape to think (B) of the scenes (C) in the movies (D).

✓ *Correction:*

7. The agency barely (A) managed to understand (B) what Sanders wanted before the contract; he (C) preferred receiving cash up front than increasing (D) the annual bonus.

✓ **Correction:**

8. Rachel felt like to wear (A) the high heels for a change (B) this morning, having been fired (C) from the job last week (D).

✓ **Correction:**

9. Nick suggested to return (A) Gorge the smart phone, but (B) I did not see the point of it unless (C) she first promised to pay (D) the fee.

✓ **Correction:**

10. Jeff suggested to (A) Emiliano that they played (B) basketball together, but (C) he already had an appointment (D).

✓ **Correction:**

PART 3 ANSWERS

1. B 把 to participate 改成 participating，reject 后应接动名词
2. A 把 to watch 改成 watching，be worth 后需要接动名词
3. A 把 to sing 改成 singing，finish 后应接动名词
4. C 把 to visit 改成 visiting，postpone 后应接动名词
5. D 把 to use 改成 using，keep 后应接动名词
6. B 把 to think 改成 thinking，escape 后应接动名词
7. D 把 than 改成 to，本句为对比，使用词组 prefer A to B
8. A 把 to wear 改成 wearing，feel like 后应接动名词
9. A 把 to return 改成 returning，suggest 后应接动名词
10. B 把 played 改成 play，动词 suggest 后接 that 引导的从句的时候，从句动词应使用 should + 原形或者直接使用动词原形，以表达建议的语气。

UNIT 2

DAY 2

DAY 3

DAY 2

PART 1 IDIOMS & EXPRESSIONS

access to 有权使用……
affection = have an effect on 影响……
a number of = many 很多
a pang of 一阵……（多指突然而强烈的情感）
as a result of 结果，因此
a stretch of 一片
at the sight of 看见……时
be accused of = accuse A of B 因……被起诉，批评
be covered with 盖着，覆着
be done with 处理，再也不……了
be known for 因……而众所周知
be known to 为……所熟知
be native to = home to 原产于……
be obsessed with 痴迷于……
be responsible for 为……负责，形成……的原因
burst into 突然开始……
in case of 万一
instead of 代替……
leave for 出发去……
long for + noun =long to + verb 渴望……
native to 原产于
refer to 指……
refrain A from B 制止 A 不让 B
result in 导致
the number of ……的数量

PART 2 BRIEF GRAMMAR FOR IDIOMS & EXPRESSIONS

介词 + 名词 = 副词

跟介词连用的名词不能用作主语或者宾语，因为这种情况已经不再具有名词的性质，而是相当于一个副词。如果已经使用了副词，就不需要在前面使用介词了。

Ex) **In the school** has many special activities to promote students' capacity.（这里的介词短语不能用作主语，需要改成 school。）

Ex) She got to know the truth **by accidently**.（这里需要将 accidently 修改成 accident，副词不能和介词连用，或者去掉介词，直接使用副词。）

DAY 3

PART 3 PRACTICE QUESTIONS

Choose an incorrect answer and write the correct form in the *Correction.*

1. Before the final term (A), Sam and Tim had determined (B) to study, but as a result from (C) the football game and the party afterward, they (D) received rather disappointing grades.

✓ *Correction:*

2. One of the benefits (A) to the area is (B) that the residents use only small stretch of (C) land so that many plots are left empty (D) for development.

✓ *Correction:*

3. Widespread (A) snow followed by strong wind can result in (B) avalanches, which have dangerous (C) affects on (D) the skiers.

✓ **Correction:**

4. Because of (A) the innocent nature, Carrie has a hard time (B) even talking (C) to someone accused with (D) lying.

✓ **Correction:**

5. When living (A) in a densely (B) packed residential area, one (C) should refrain of playing (D) loud music.

✓ **Correction:**

6. Drivers should be careful (A) not to use the brake often on (B) a road covered by snow (C) because cars have a tendency to slip (D) when they hit the brake.

✓ **Correction:**

7. Phillip, not native English speaker, who (A) has taught two years (B) in Vietnam, is well (C) known by his teaching skills (D).

✓ **Correction:**

8. The access code toward (A) the wireless network (B) of the school is (C) well known to (D) the students.

✓ **Correction:**

9. A number of students, even though (A) they know (B) the deadline of Physics homework, long to (C) the extension since most of them had to leave for (D) a field study.

✓ **Correction:**

10. The number of students, who knew the deadline of the Physics homework, were very small that the professor might not have said it clearly.
(A: of students; B: who knew; C: were; D: clearly)

✓ **Correction:**

11. We are very obsessive with success, which is often unreachable.
(A: obsessive; B: success; C: is; D: unreachable)

✓ **Correction:**

12. She is longing for to buy a new skirt, since it is getting warmer and time to get a job.
(A: is longing; B: for to buy; C: since; D: time)

✓ **Correction:**

13. Alexandra cried in the sight of sick dolphins, which were under the state preservation program.
(A: cried in; B: dolphins, which; C: under; D: state)

✓ **Correction:**

14. When Jerry watched his food grinding in rapidly with Rosie's, he suddenly burst into tears.
(A: grinding in rapidly; B: Rosie's; C: burst; D: tears)

✓ **Correction:**

15. The spraying paint changed the color of the wall to green instead blue.
(A: spraying; B: the color of; C: to green; D: instead blue)

✓ **Correction:**

16. A couple of months ago she said she was done to date the senior student, but I saw them together in the cinema yesterday.
(A: A couple of months ago; B: said; C: done to date; D: them)

✓ **Correction:**

17. Since the sight of the beggar she saw yesterday, Elizabeth has felt a pang of guilty.
(A: Since; B: she saw yesterday; C: has felt; D: a pang of guilty)

✓ **Correction:**

18. Kim referred many expressions when she was working on her term paper on the 18th century English literature.

A B C D

✓ **Correction:**

19. When you are stung by a wild bee, you should identify which bee is responsible to the wound in case of an allergic reaction.

A B C D

✓ **Correction:**

20. Of 200 snake species native within Japan, only 2 percent are fatal to humans.

A B C D

✓ **Correction:**

PART 4 ANSWERS

1. C 把 from 改成 of
2. C 加入不定冠词 a，形成词组 a small stretch of
3. D 把 affects 改成 effects
4. D 把 with 改成 of
5. D 把 of 改成 from
6. C 把 by 改成 with
7. D 把 by 改成 for
8. A 把 toward 改成 to
9. C 把 to 改成 for

   通常 to 后接动词，而 for 后接名词，但不绝对。
10. C 把 were 改成 was

    当使用 the number of 的时候，主语为 number，所以做如上修改。
11. A 把 obsessive 改成 obsessed
12. B 把 for to buy 改成 to buy 或者 for

    for 的介词宾语为 a new skirt，而不是 to buy a new skirt，因此做如上改动。
13. A 把 in 改成 at
14. A 把 grinding in rapidly 改成 to rapidly grinding

    in 后不能接副词，因此做如上修改。
15. D 把 instead blue 改成 instead of blue
16. C 把 done to date 改成 done with dating
17. D 把 a pang of guilty 改成 a pang of guilt

    guilty 是形容词，不能在这里使用。
18. A refer 后应接 to 以构成短语 refer to
19. C 把 to 改成 for
20. B 把 within 改成 to

UNIT 3

DAY 4

PART 1 IDIOMS & EXPRESSIONS

PART 2 BRIEF GRAMMAR FOR IDIOMS & EXPRESSIONS

DAY 5

PART 3 PRACTICE QUESTIONS

PART 4 ANSWERS

DAY 4

PART 1 IDIOMS & EXPRESSIONS

acclimate (oneself) to + noun 使……适应……
adjust (oneself) to + noun 调整……以适应……
at hand 在手边，在附近，即将来临或者发生
in hand 在手中
on hand 在手边，在附近，可用
be aware of 意识到，知道
be concerned about 关心，挂念
be concerned with 参与，干预
be famous for = renowned for 因……而著名
be filled with 充满着，怀着
be interested in 对……感兴趣
be known as 号称……，被认为是……（这里后面多接某种职业）
be known to be 被称为，被叫作（这里后面多接某种处境）
be likely to 可能
be opposed to(opposite to/ oppose) 反对……
be willing to 愿意……
be worried about(worry about) 为……忧虑
by(in) virtue of 凭借……的力量，由于
in an effort to 企图……，努力……
in one's(the) way 阻碍某人
it is not until... that 直到……才
liken A to B 把 A 比作 B
not only A but also B 不但 A……而且 B……
on foot 步行
on one's(the) way 在……的路上
partake in=take part in=participate in 参与，参加

put forth 放出，发表
put on hold 搁置，延期
search for 寻找
suffer from 受……的折磨，因……而遭受痛苦
suffer through 遭受，挨过
transfer to 转学到……， 转移到……

PART 2 BRIEF GRAMMAR FOR IDIOMS & EXPRESSIONS

1. It was not until... that 直到……才

这种结构一般用于强调，最原始的句子是这样的：

Ex) Johnson did **not get** a car accident and is not sure that he can play in this season **until** his foot got better from the injury from the last season.

把 not 和 until 放在一起句子可以转换成如下的形式：

Ex) **Not until** his foot got better from the injury from the last season **did Johnson get** a car accident and is not sure that he can play in this season. (这种形式也十分常用)

最后，前面使用 it is (was)... that, 这样这个句子就变成了一个强调句。

Ex) **It was not until** his foot got better from the injury from the last season **that** Johnson **got** a car accident and is not sure that he can play in this season.

2. 动词 +to 形式

动词不定式在这里并不是作为名词性词组或者补语的功能出现。

Ex) She **was to call** her parents about the engagement.

在这种情况下，动词前面的 be to 可译成“能、将要、应该、想要或指定”等。

Ex) Hiroki **was to sleep**, but his roommate suddenly woke him up.

这里 was to 的意思是“想要……”。

DAY 5

PART 3 PRACTICE QUESTIONS

Choose an incorrect answer and write the correct form in the *Correction.*

1. Most nocturnal animals hide during the day (A) and search (B) food at night to save energy by avoiding (C) the heat and to hide (D) themselves from predators.

   ✓ ***Correction:***

2. China has many of the most (A) advanced technologies ready (B) to be used in the hand (C) but some (D) need to be tested more.

   ✓ ***Correction:***

3. When you mortgage (A) your home, you should be aware about (B) the terms the bank puts forth (C); otherwise (D), you should pay the higher interest rate.

   ✓ ***Correction:***

4. The emergency room was filled of (A) doctors wanting (B) to see the rare patient, who (C) had the green mole on the shoulder (D).

   ✓ ***Correction:***

5. James, who has never participated in (A) any official race, goes to school by foot (B) every day in an effort to train (C) himself for a track race (D).

   ✓ ***Correction:***

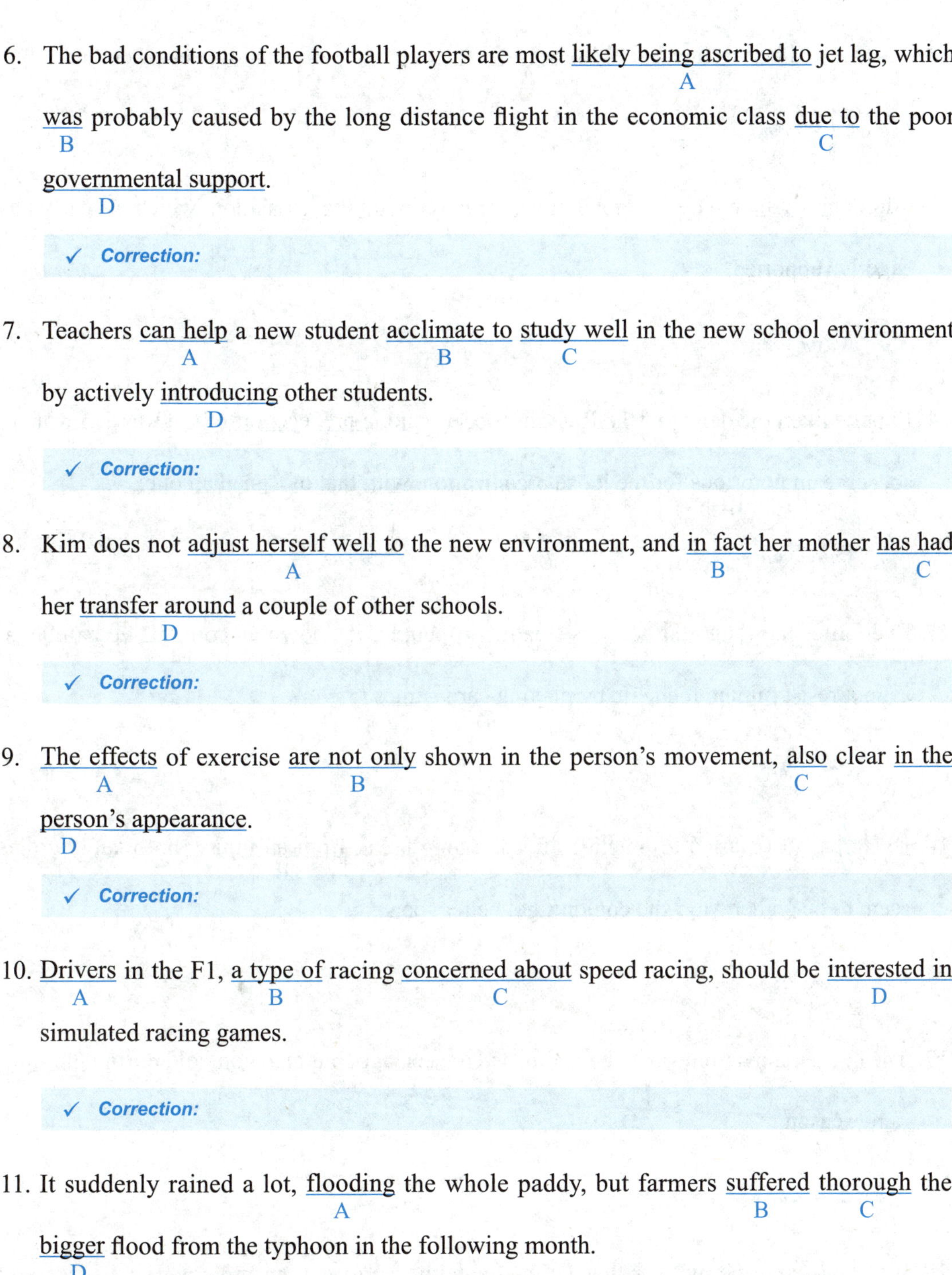

6. The bad conditions of the football players are most <u>likely being ascribed to</u> (A) jet lag, which <u>was</u> (B) probably caused by the long distance flight in the economic class <u>due to</u> (C) the poor <u>governmental support</u> (D).

✓ **Correction:**

7. Teachers <u>can help</u> (A) a new student <u>acclimate to</u> (B) <u>study well</u> (C) in the new school environment by actively <u>introducing</u> (D) other students.

✓ **Correction:**

8. Kim does not <u>adjust herself well to</u> (A) the new environment, and <u>in fact</u> (B) her mother <u>has had</u> (C) her <u>transfer around</u> (D) a couple of other schools.

✓ **Correction:**

9. <u>The effects</u> (A) of exercise <u>are not only</u> (B) shown in the person's movement, <u>also</u> clear <u>in the</u> (C) <u>person's appearance</u> (D).

✓ **Correction:**

10. <u>Drivers</u> (A) in the F1, <u>a type of</u> (B) racing <u>concerned about</u> (C) speed racing, should be <u>interested in</u> (D) simulated racing games.

✓ **Correction:**

11. It suddenly rained a lot, <u>flooding</u> (A) the whole paddy, but farmers <u>suffered</u> (B) <u>thorough</u> (C) the <u>bigger</u> (D) flood from the typhoon in the following month.

✓ **Correction:**

12. Susan asked her brother Sam if he was willing to partake the school talent show.
(A: asked; B: her brother Sam; C: was willing to; D: partake the school)

✓ Correction:

13. I don't understand why Senator Jim was opposed with the legislation, which his party has eagerly supported.
(A: don't understand; B: was opposed with; C: which; D: has eagerly)

✓ Correction:

14. Experts liken the defeat of the Russian soccer team, a predecessor of the Russian woman soccer team notorious for the loose organization, with that of Canadian one.
(A: team, a predecessor; B: notorious for; C: with; D: of Canadian one)

✓ Correction:

15. Even after the long and arduous treatment, people, if known as compulsive gamblers, cannot resist ruining their life by playing card games.
(A: long and arduous; B: known as; C: resist ruining; D: playing card games)

✓ Correction:

16. Daisy has just started to practice after the long break from an injury, but many hurdles seem to be on her way; she couldn't get better soon.
(A: has just started; B: from an injury; C: many hurdles; D: on her way)

✓ Correction:

17. The house renovation was to have finished a week ago, but taken on hold during the short rainy season.
(A: was to; B: a week ago; C: taken on hold; D: the short rainy season)

✓ Correction:

18. It was not until he met her that Jay had any chance of getting promoted and successful for his job.
(A: met; B: that Jay had; C: any chance; D: for)

✓ Correction:

19. Although worried not coming back on time to work on Monday, Pam anyways planned for the trip to Central America.
(A: worried; B: not coming back; C: Pam anyways planned; D: for ... Central America)

✓ **Correction:**

20. By the virtue of his intelligence and charm, Alex could successfully become the captain of the debating club.
(A: By the virtue of; B: intelligence and charm; C: could successfully become; D: the captain)

✓ **Correction:**

PART 4 ANSWERS

1. B 为了表达寻找的意图，需要使用词组 search for
2. C 去掉 the
3. B 把 about 改成 of
4. A 把 of 改成 with
5. B 把 by 改成 on
6. A 把 being 改成 to be
7. C 把 study 改成 studying
8. D 把 around 改成 to
9. C 把 also 改成 but also 或者 but
10. C 把 about 改成 with
11. C 把 thorough 改成 through
12. D 在 partake 后加入介词 in
13. B 把 with 改成 to
14. C 把 with 改成 to
15. B 把 as 改成 to be

    后应该连接某种职业或者工作，而这里赌徒并不是任何职业，相反可以理解成一种状况或者一种处境，因此做以上的修改。
16. D 把 on 改成 in

    词组 in the way 意为阻止，而 on the way 则意为在途中，因此做如上修改。
17. C 把 taken 改成 put
18. D 把 for 改成 in
19. A 在 worried 后加入 about，构成短语 worry about
20. A 去掉 the，构成短语 by virtue of

UNIT 4

DAY 6

PART 1 IDIOMS & EXPRESSIONS

PART 2 BRIEF GRAMMAR FOR IDIOMS & EXPRESSIONS

DAY 7

PART 3 PRACTICE QUESTIONS

PART 4 ANSWERS

DAY 6

PART 1 IDIOMS & EXPRESSIONS

a series of 一系列，一连串
at one's fingertips 近在手边，随时可用
be accessible to 可接近，可用
be accustomed to (be used to) ...ing 习惯于……
be in contract with 与……保持联络
be indifferent to/about 对…… 不关心
be inferior to 次于……
be superior to 优于……
be junior to 比……年轻，次
be senior to 比……年长，优
be ill at ease 局促不安，心神不宁
be involved in 涉及，卷入，参与
by deadline 截止
come into existence 成立，建立
consist of (be composed of) 由……组成
dispossess A of B 剥夺 A 对 B 的权利，从 A 那里夺走 B
rid A of B 使 A 不能拥有 B
rob A of B 从 A 手里抢走 B
either A or B 要么 A，要么 B……
neither A nor B A 或者 B 都不……
engage in 参与，从事，忙于……
hands-on 亲身实践的，实际动手操作的
in favor of 赞成或者支持某人或某事
in spite of 虽然，尽管……, 不顾……
no sooner... than... 一……就……
object to noun/...ing 反对，对……反感

preoccupation with 全神贯注于……
prefer to 更喜欢……，宁愿……
put at ease 使不拘束（不紧张），使安心
take into account 将……考虑在内

PART 2 BRIEF GRAMMAR FOR IDIOMS & EXPRESSIONS

1. 使用 to 代替 than 进行比较的情况

inferior to, superior to, junior to, senior to, prefer to

以上几个词组不可使用 than 进行比较。

Ex) John was dominating the game; he was much inferior **than** the opponent. (错误：这里不能使用 than，需要替换成 to。)

Ex) John was inferior to the opponent. (正确)

2. No sooner ... than...

No sooner 引导的句子里的动作需要发生在 than 引导的部分之前。典型的句子顺序应该如下：no sooner + 主语 + had + 过去分词（过去完成时）+ than + 主语 + 过去式

Ex) **No sooner** Tim **had used** the fountain pen **than** his supervisor, who was passing and saw him using it, **confiscated** it because fountain pens were banned in the company.

3. 用来连接句子时连词、副词和介词的使用

▲ **连词用来连接两个完整的句子，但是前后两个句子有重复的部分可以进行省略处理。**

最基本连词：that

并列连词：and, but, or, nor, so, yet

表原因的连词：because, as, since, in that

表条件的连词：if, unless, in case, providing, provided that

表让步的连词：although, even though, even if, though

表时间的连词：when, while, every time, as, until, till, since, by the time, before, after

Ex) Sally does not get along well with her **colleagues**, **she** is afraid of talking to people. (错误：这个句子当中需要连词 because 进行连接，而不能单独使用逗号。)

Ex) I agree with the statement. Because cars make noises and roads are getting congested. (错误：Because 是连词，因此不能在单一的句子中使用，所以需要做如下修改：I agree with the **statement because** cars make noises and roads are getting congested.)

▲ **副词不能够用来连接完整的句子，而连词则可以。请注意下面这些副词与连词的区别。**

however, nevertheless, nonetheless, still

accordingly, consequently, hence, therefore, thus, as a result, finally

besides, furthermore, moreover, above all, in addition

indeed, in fact

then, thereafter

contrarily, in contrast

otherwise

meantime, meanwhile, by the way

▲ **介词短语并非句子，介词后接名词或者动名词，故在句子中出现的介词短语，并不需要使用连词与主句进行连接。以下的介词短语需要接名词或者动名词。**

according to, in case of

because of, thanks to, due to, owing to

concerning, regarding, respecting

despite, in spite of

during

irrespective of, regardless of

instead of, rather than, including

such as, like

Ex) **Due to** Claris did not tell the truth, the whole mission stopped. (错误：“due to”后不能接句子。在这里把 due to 改成 because，或者改成 **Due to Claris who** did not tell the truth。)

Ex) **Despite** the van broke down, Michael was not discouraged. (错误：把 Despite the van broke down 改成 **Despite the broken van**，因为介词后必须接名词或名词词组而不是句子)

4. Either A or B/Neither A nor B

这两个需要遵循就近原则，动词的数要根据就近的主语进行判断。

Ex) Either the cars or the train **go** there. (错误：go 应该跟与它就近的主语的数统一，因此这里修改成 goes。)

DAY 7

PART 3 PRACTICE QUESTIONS

Choose an incorrect answer and write the correct form in the *Correction.*

1. It had long been believed (A) that the last comma at the end of (B) series of (C) words should be put when the grammar rules came into existence (D) in modern British dictionaries.

   ✓ *Correction:*

2. Having been slow (A) to comprehend his brother's preoccupation on (B) learning German, Joshua was surprised to hear (C) that his family might have to (D) move to Germany.

   ✓ *Correction:*

3. Either the whole members or (A) John alone are responsible for (B) the collaborating work between (C) the two schools, which was not done by deadline (D).

   ✓ *Correction:*

4. Having waited (A) for an hour, Chris pretended to be (B) indifferent with (C) Tom, since he could look vulnerable (D) by showing anger.

   ✓ *Correction:*

5. In the beginning of the war, the Japanese army was (A) superior not only in weapons, but also (B) in tactics than (C) those of other countries (D) in the region.

   ✓ *Correction:*

6. No sooner Rachel joined (A) the new agency to prepare (B) for international competition than (C) her old agency sued her for breaking the contract (D).

✓ **Correction:**

7. The way (A) she treats people makes (B) everyone (C) in the room ill at easy (D).

✓ **Correction:**

8. Clayton's warm smile and sense of (A) humor put his students in ease (B) during the class that he can approach each problem (C) very closely (D).

✓ **Correction:**

9. In spite of (A) the innate (B) physical advantages, Woods could conquer (C) many international competitions (D).

✓ **Correction:**

10. My mother's zeal (A) support in favor for (B) longer school hours has often engaged family members in (C) the heated (D) discussion.

✓ **Correction:**

11. Young children (A) can develop their motor and perceptual skills (B) with hand-on (C) hobbies (D).

✓ **Correction:**

12. Ms. Jenna seems to have (A) all chemistry knowledge in her fingertips (B); she doesn't even hesitate and supports (C) firmly for her stance (D) when she is challenged by students with fairly advanced questions.

✓ **Correction:**

13. The last resort (A) to rid his cat Mendel fleas (B) is to shave completely (C), but nobody in the pet

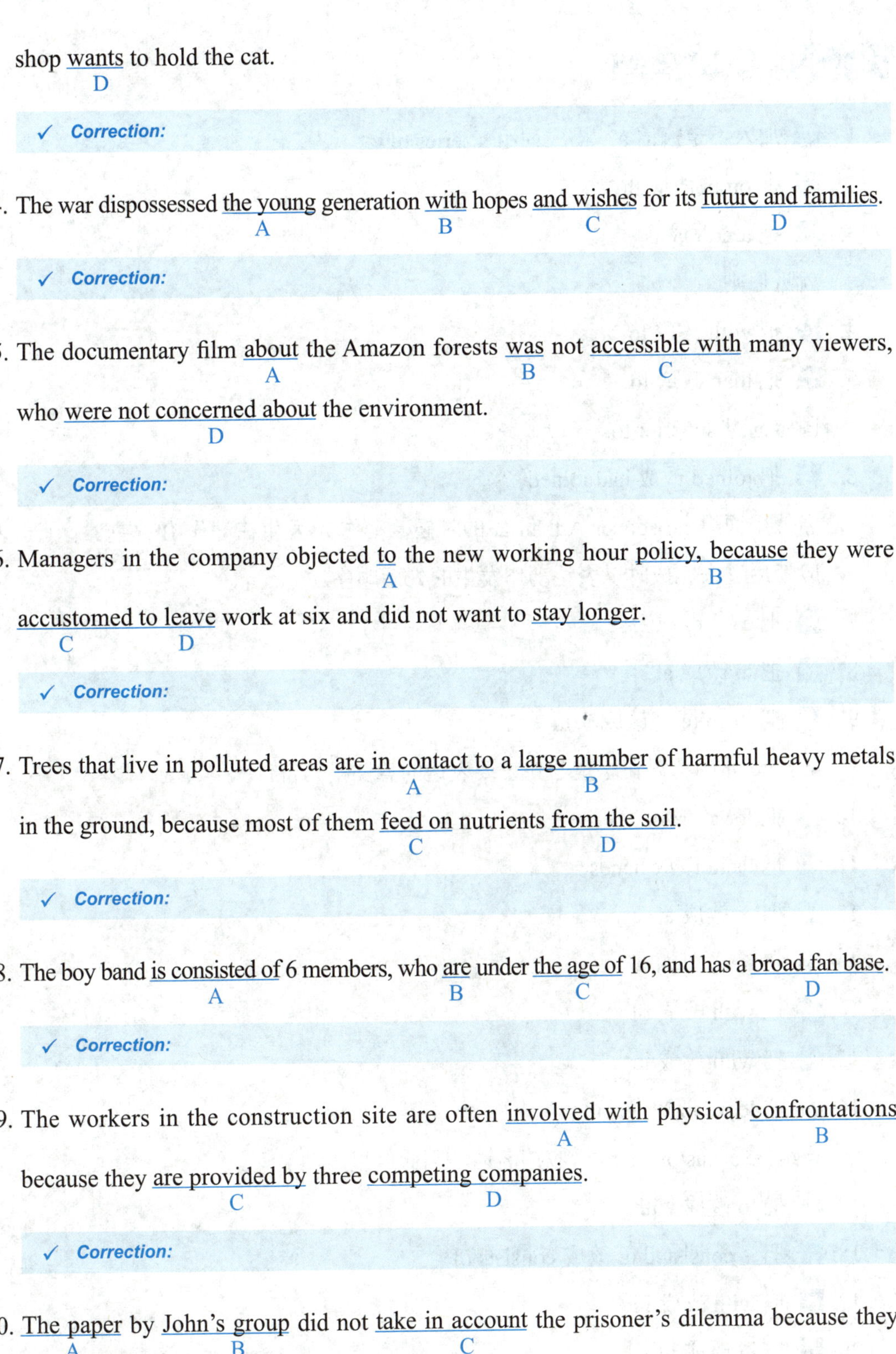

shop wants (D) to hold the cat.

✓ **Correction:**

14. The war dispossessed the young (A) generation with (B) hopes and wishes (C) for its future and families (D).

✓ **Correction:**

15. The documentary film about (A) the Amazon forests was (B) not accessible with (C) many viewers, who were not concerned about (D) the environment.

✓ **Correction:**

16. Managers in the company objected to (A) the new working hour policy, because (B) they were accustomed (C) to leave (D) work at six and did not want to stay longer.

✓ **Correction:**

17. Trees that live in polluted areas are in contact to (A) a large number (B) of harmful heavy metals in the ground, because most of them feed on (C) nutrients from the soil (D).

✓ **Correction:**

18. The boy band is consisted of (A) 6 members, who are (B) under the age of (C) 16, and has a broad fan base (D).

✓ **Correction:**

19. The workers in the construction site are often involved with (A) physical confrontations (B) because they are provided by (C) three competing companies (D).

✓ **Correction:**

20. The paper (A) by John's group (B) did not take in account (C) the prisoner's dilemma because they dealt with the social structure of orangutans (D).

✓ **Correction:**

PART 4 ANSWERS

1. C 加入不定冠词 a，构成词组 a series of
2. B 把 on 改成 with
3. B 把 are 改成 is

   就近原则。
4. C 把 with 改成 to
5. C 把 than 改成 to

   固定词组 superior to。
6. A 把 joined 改成 had joined

   当使用词组 no sooner A than B 的时候，动作 A 发生在动作 B 之前，因此这里应使用过去完成时以表达动作发生的先后顺序。
7. D 把 easy 改成 ease
8. B 把 in 改成 at
9. A 把 In spite of 改成 With

   in spite of 的意思在这里与句子要表达的意图不相符。
10. B 把 for 改成 of
11. C 把 hand 改成 hands
12. B 把 in 改成 at
13. B 在 fleas 前加 of
14. B 把 with 改成 of
15. C 把 with 改成 to
16. C 把 leave 改成 leaving

    词组 be accustomed to 后应接名词，因此这里用动名词。
17. A 把 to 改成 with
18. A 把 is consisted of 改成 consists of
19. A 把 with 改成 in
20. C 把 in 改成 into

UNIT 5

DAY 8

PART 1 IDIOMS & EXPRESSIONS

PART 2 BRIEF GRAMMAR FOR IDIOMS & EXPRESSIONS

DAY 9

PART 3 PRACTICE QUESTIONS

PART 4 ANSWERS

DAY 8

PART 1 IDIOMS & EXPRESSIONS

as well as 也，又
at the sight of 看见……时
attribute ... to 把某事归因于……
be able to (have an ability to) 能……
be acceptable to 对……可以接受
be capable of (have a capacity of) 能……
be equivalent to 相等或相当于……
be fond of 喜欢……
be harmful to someone 对某人有害
be helpful for something or someone 对某人或某事有利
be likely to (be unlikely to) 很可能……
be made of 用……制成
be made from 由……去掉做成（多用于原材料不易看出的情况）
be made up of 由……组成
be sure of 确信
cannot help... doing 不得不
cannot help but 只能
come across 偶然发现，偶然遇到
come to a conclusion 得出结论
contribute to 促成，捐献
deal with 处理，应付
despite 尽管，虽然
differ from (be different from) 与……不同
give a break 休息一下
give way to 给……让路
have no choice but to 只能……

in vain 白费地，徒劳地
look forward to 期望，盼望
look into 考察，调查，研究
look to 指望，依靠
make friends with 与……交朋友
pay for 为……付钱
red-handed 当场抓住，当场逮获
see ... off 送行，送别
succeed in 在……中获得成功
succeed to 继承，继任
to one's surprise 让……吃惊

PART 2 BRIEF GRAMMAR FOR IDIOMS & EXPRESSIONS

1. 'Pay for' VS 'Pay'

Pay：接一定金额的钱或者某人

Ex) She has to **pay** $15.

Ex) Mary needs to **pay** Cathy.

Pay for：接某种服务或者工作 / 接借来的东西

Ex) Tom **paid for** the vacation for his family.

Ex) Norton **paid for** fixing his computer.

Ex) David **paid** ￥300 **for** the debt.

2. 'A as well as B'

这个词组在使用的时候需要关注前后的统一，
当词组后面接动词的时候，动词的数应与A保持一致。
Ex) **The cat** as well as the dogs **are** in perfect conditions. (错误，需要将 are 改成 is)

DAY 9

PART 3 PRACTICE QUESTIONS

Choose an incorrect answer and write the correct form in the *Correction.*

1. The movie was not acceptable to (A) many Israelis (B), who found some scenes very offensive in dealing historical (C) background of their (D) country and religion.

   ✓ ***Correction:***

2. The recent expedition of the space probe sent (A) many beautiful pictures of landscapes (B) of the other planets (C) that comprise of (D) the solar system.

   ✓ ***Correction:***

3. Happiness is not equivalent with (A) money; happiness (B) cannot be made while (C) money can be achieved (D).

   ✓ ***Correction:***

4. Despite she is (A) outgoing, Suzi has difficulty making (B) friends with (C) Dr. Hammel because of (D) his shyness.

   ✓ ***Correction:***

5. Hanna has an ability of persuading (A) in a very hard position; she was able to (B) make her mother support (C) her after failing (D) the same business twice.

   ✓ ***Correction:***

6. Ray was not capable of paying his debt back to his friends, who had no choice but to call his father.
(A: capable of; B: paying; C: his friends, who; D: but to)

✓ Correction:

7. Dr. Yamaha could not help laugh at the sight of Steve; he had been walking around the campus with the graffiti on the forehead.
(A: help laugh; B: at the sight of; C: had been walking; D: on the forehead)

✓ Correction:

8. The success of her school is attributed in part to Adam, the math teacher, who contributed to increase the reputation.
(A: is attributed; B: to Adam; C: who; D: to increase)

✓ Correction:

9. Most parents believe that smart phones are not harmful for their children, since they are helpful for brain activity.
(A: Most parents; B: harmful for; C: since; D: for brain activity)

✓ Correction:

10. To hers surprise, Mike, who had never taken care of house choirs, voluntarily said he would look into why TV was not working.
(A: To hers surprise; B: had never taken; C: look into; D: why)

✓ Correction:

11. Gerry's parents were looking forward to see the Math teacher, who did not look to his potential weaknesses.
(A: were looking forward to see; B: who; C: look to; D: weaknesses)

✓ Correction:

12. Lisa was fond to look up the dictionary even when she was pretty sure of the accuracy of words and sentences.
(A: to look; B: even when; C: sure of; D: words and sentences)

✓ Correction:

13. Pagers were quickly giving a way to (A) cell-phones at the end of 1990s (B) and today they (C) are used mostly (D) by doctors and criminals.

✓ **Correction:**

14. The metal sculpture was made mainly by iron (A) and thus (B) we cannot display it (C) outside because it will become rusty (D).

✓ **Correction:**

15. The corrupted (A) bodies were observed (B) by him as (C) they succeeded in (D) the source of life.

✓ **Correction:**

16. The frogs most likely to (A) survive the rainy season (B), and after the season (C) their population will unstoppably increase (D).

✓ **Correction:**

17. Zack wrote (A) the letter of plea in the vain (B) because he had got caught red-handed (C) and the police (D) would not give him any break.

✓ **Correction:**

18. What she told us about his behavior differed with (A) his claim that (B) he was very generous (C) towards his family (D).

✓ **Correction:**

19. When I went to the airport to see her off (A), I came cross (B) a group of Japanese tourists, who had no idea of (C) where to catch a cab (D).

✓ **Correction:**

20. Denny, who <u>has just graduated</u>, as well as his brothers, <u>who have</u> many years of
A B
experience <u>in the field of</u> chemical engineering, <u>have come to</u> the conclusion that
C D
working in the same company should not be the best option.

✓ ***Correction:***

PART 4 ANSWERS

1. C 在 historical 前加入 with
2. D 去掉介词 of
   comprise 后不需要接介词。
3. A 把 with 改成 to
4. A 把 she is 改成 being
   despite 不能引导句子，后应接名词。
5. A 把 of persuading 改成 to persuade
6. B 在 paying 后加入 for 构成词组
7. A 把 laugh 改成 laughing
   在 can/could not help 后需使用动名词。
8. D 把 increase 改成 increasing
   在 contribute to 后应使用动名词。
9. B 把 for 改成 to
10. A 把 hers 改成 her
    to one's surprise 为固定词组。
11. A 把 see 改成 seeing
    词组 look forward to 后应使用动名词。
12. A 把 to look 改成 of looking
13. A 去掉不定冠词 a
    正确的词组应该是 give way to。
14. A 把 by 改成 of
15. D 把 in 改成 to
    succeed in 意为在某领域或事情上成功，但是 succeed to 则意为继续。
16. A 改成 Frogs are likely to
17. B 去掉定冠词 the
18. A 把 with 改成 from
19. B 把 cross 改成 across
20. D 把 have 改成 has
    当使用 A as well as B 这一结构的时候，动词的数应以 A 为准。

UNIT 6

DAY 10

DAY 11

DAY 10

PART 1 IDIOMS & EXPRESSIONS

account for（数量或者比例上）占，导致，解释
at large 在逃
be familiar with / to (familiarize a with b) 熟悉……
be negligent of (about) 在……上存在疏漏
be oblivious of 忘记了……
be oblivious to 没有注意到，没有察觉到
be regarded as 被视为……
be regarded to be 被认为是……
be satisfied with 对……满意
by order of 奉……的命令
call off 取消
contrary to 与……相反
delve into 钻研，深入研究
in need of 需要
in pursuit of 追求……，寻求……
in time 及时
on time 按时，准时
just as..., so 正像…… 也……
hand in (turn in) 上交，递交
hand out 分布，散发
participate in 参与，参加
pay attention to 关注
put out 伸出，扑灭，出版
put off 推迟，拖延
put away 把……收起，放好
search for 搜索，搜寻
similar to 与……相似

thanks to (due to, owing to) 幸亏，多亏
under (the) control of 在……的控制之下

PART 2 BRIEF GRAMMAR FOR IDIOMS & EXPRESSIONS

1. familiar with VS familiar to

Familiar with：当人作主语的时候意为习惯于或者熟知……

Ex) Nancy **is familiar with** the military system because her boyfriend is in the army.

Ex) Ellen **is familiar with** people in the park since she goes there every day.

Familiar to：无论句子中的主语是人或者物，to 的宾语只能是人

Ex) The sitcom **was familiar to most of Indians** because one of the characters is an Indian.

2. oblivious of VS oblivious to

Oblivious of：这个相当于忘记了……

Ex) He was becoming **oblivious of** details of work schedule that he hired an assistant.

Oblivious to：对于形势或者环境反应迟钝，不敏感或者不了解

Ex) Mark **was oblivious to** the Vietnamese war because he was in the coma.

3. by and method

当使用介词 by 的时候，句子表示使用的方法或者工具，接的名词前不需要使用任何冠词。

Ex) Mel often talks to his parents **by webcam**. (这里不可以使用冠词)

4. just as..., so (too)

这并不是常见的 as...as 的对比，‘Just as’ 相当于连词连接两个句子，很多同学认为第二个句子不再需要任何连词，但是在这种情况下句首的 so 或者 too 是必要的，实际上 just as...so 在语法上属于连词当中的关联连词，与我们很熟悉的 neither...nor 等的用法相同，必须成对出现。

Ex) **Just as** Tomoko thinks of his family while away from home, his family misses him and talks about him every day. (错误 ，需要在逗号与 his family 之间插入 so(too))

Ex) **Just as** many western cultures don’t believe eastern way of treating diseases, **so** many old people in China still depend on their traditional ways of Chinese medicine and acupuncture. (正确)

DAY 11

PART 3 PRACTICE QUESTIONS

Choose an incorrect answer and write the correct form in the *Correction.*

1. As (A) I was familiar to (B) the painting, the painter was also (C) familiar to (D) me.

   ✓ **Correction:**

2. Thanks to (A) Julie's sister, we could enter the test center on time (B) and have some time to calm ourselves (C) down before the test (D).

   ✓ **Correction:**

3. John is regarded to be (A) one of the most talented dancers (B) in his school and often asked (C) to participate in (D) concerts of school bands.

   ✓ **Correction:**

4. Just as the other Asian teams (A), such as Iranian and Japanese soccer team, lost all the matches in the first round in the world cup, Korean (B) team was (C) eliminated in the first round (D).

   ✓ **Correction:**

5. Clara was more satisfied at (A) her son's decision than his choice of major (B), because (C) she had been worried that he would (D) be very indecisive about the future.

   ✓ **Correction:**

6. In large for more than three days, the deserter has been believed to hide in one of the mountains around his army camp or cross the border line.
(A: In large; B: has been believed; C: mountains; D: cross the border line)

✓ **Correction:**

7. Suzie was certain that she was going to get an A in history, because she handed for an extra paper for additional reading.
(A: was certain that; B: get an A; C: handed for; D: additional reading)

✓ **Correction:**

8. Professor Hue does not hand in homework often, and this is the biggest reason his lectures are often full.
(A: hand in; B: often; C: the biggest reason; D: are often full)

✓ **Correction:**

9. When she arrived at the meeting, most agendas had been already dealt with, but the rest of the board members still wanted her to account about some of the agendas.
(A: had been; B: dealt with; C: board members; D: account about)

✓ **Correction:**

10. Even though he looked very suspicious, the detectives could not continue any more, and decided to get the warrant to search for his house.
(A: Even though; B: the detectives; C: decided; D: search for)

✓ **Correction:**

11. Finding Japanese similar with his native language, Zhang changed his mind and decided to study English first, since he believed accomplishing something more difficult would save him more time for something easier like Japanese.
(A: Finding; B: similar with; C: changed his mind and decided to; D: accomplishing)

✓ **Correction:**

12. Joana and her fiancé are meeting with (A) their parents from both sides (B) to discuss about (C) financial issues (D) for their marriage such as how big the house should be and what kind of furniture it should have.

✓ **Correction:**

13. By the order of (A) the chief of police department of New York, the chaos, seeming (B) impossible to control, was fast and effectively (C) getting under control (D).

✓ **Correction:**

14. Most citizens are now oblivious with (A) the accident, which took away over 200 lives, but the radio station has still been keeping up with (B) the news of it (C) every morning (D).

✓ **Correction:**

15. After many big disasters caused by (A) corruption and loose monitoring system (B), most citizens in the country have become oblivious of (C) the insecure (D) surroundings.

✓ **Correction:**

16. Most expatriates in pursuit for (A) jobs outside their own countries (B) should prove that they have bachelor degrees (C) and no history of (D) criminal activity.

✓ **Correction:**

17. Even though Jose zealously endeavors to supplant the corn based oil (A) with fish based one, the investment for the study is likely to (B) be called off (C), and he will have to put out (D) the study until he finds another investor.

✓ **Correction:**

18. Jen was not <u>negligent to</u> (A) cleaning her dorm room, <u>but</u> (B) she was rather disorganized that after <u>putting away</u> (C) her stuff from the couch, the room looked as clean as <u>any normal girl's</u> (D).

✓ **Correction:**

19. <u>Contrary to</u> (A) the praises that the futuristic novel, 2001: A space odyssey, <u>delved religious and philosophical aspects</u> (B) of fear and anxiety, Stephen does not like the book because the ending part <u>seems to him</u> (C) just an easy way <u>to end</u> (D) the story the author could not handle.

✓ **Correction:**

20. Negative <u>effects of</u> (A) consuming excessive sugar <u>have been</u> (B) greatly emphasized, but modern people are actually <u>in</u> (C) need of <u>paying attention for</u> (D) consuming excessive salt to keep healthier body.

✓ **Correction:**

PART 4 ANSWERS

1. B 把 to 改成 with

   词组 be familiar with 的介词宾语既可以是人也可以是物，但是词组 be familiar to 的介词宾语却只能是人。

2. B 把 on 改成 in

   on time 表示刚好准时，所以如果使用 on time 则没有时间 calm down。

3. A 把 to be 改成 as

   to be 可以用来解释情况，但是如果使用 as 则表示某种工作或者职务。

4. B 在 Korean 前加入 so（too）

   just as ...，so 固定词组

5. A 把 at 改成 with
6. A 把 In 改成 At
7. C 把 for 改成 in
8. A 把 in 改成 out
9. D 把 about 改成 for
10. D 去掉介词 for

    search 意为仔细检查，而 search for 则意为寻找。

11. B 把 with 改成 to
12. C 去掉介词 about

    discuss 后不需要接介词

13. A 去掉定冠词 the
14. A 把 with 改成 of

    词组 be oblivious of... 意为忘记

15. C 把 of 改成 to

    be oblivious to 意为熟悉

16. A 把 for 改成 of
17. D 把 out 改成 off
18. A 把 to 改成 of
19. B 在 delved 后加入 into
20. D 把 for 改为 to pay attention to...ing 为固定词组

UNIT 7

DAY 12

DAY 13

DAY 12

PART 1 IDIOMS & EXPRESSIONS

abide by 遵守，信守
argue against 不赞成……
argue with 与……争辩
attempt to 尝试，企图
be associated with 与……联系在一起
be covered with 被……掩盖
be engaged in 从事于……
be fed up with 饱受……，厌烦……
be filled with 充满着……，怀着……
be full of 充满……
be made into 被制成……
be made of (from) 由……制成
be supposed to 应该，被期望……
depend on (upon) (rely on, count on) 依靠……，由……决定
enter into 加入（讨论）；订立（协议）；开始（关系）
insist on (insistence on) 坚持，强调……
only to 不料竟然……，没想到会……
prey on 捕食，掠夺
qualify for 有……资格
regardless of 不管……，不顾……
return to 返回到……

PART 2 BRIEF GRAMMAR FOR IDIOMS & EXPRESSIONS

“,” 逗号

使用逗号的情况

三个或三个以上事物的排列

Ex) Denis bought a shirt, a short, and a jacket.

Ex) Denis bought a shirt, a short and a jacket. (错误，在汉语中使用“和”的时候不再需要使用逗号，但是这种用法在英文中是错误的。)

在两个不同的限定语中间使用

Ex) Jenny was upset because of the boring, purposeless seminar.

当插入部分不是关键信息，而是辅助信息的时候 (读者已经知道这些信息了。)

Ex) Tim, math teacher, finally had to wake up the student.

关于逗号使用的一些误区

逗号不可以连接句子，在连接两个完整句子的时候需要额外使用连词。

Ex) Mom went out to meet her **friends**, **my** sister has not come back from school. (这个句子的逗号之后需要使用连词。)

两个事物之间使用 and 的时候可以不用逗号，但是两个事物之间使用的是 but、so 或者 or 的时候，通常需要使用逗号。

Ex) In spite of rain, **Harry and Sue** went to swim in the sea. (这里不需要使用逗号。)

Ex) The DVD player did not **work**, **but** we could watch movies with the computer.

两个不同的句子分别拥有各自的主语，中间用 and 连接，必须使用逗号。

Ex) Jan visited her **father**, **and** Suzi cleaned the house last Sunday. (两个不同的主语，需要使用逗号。)

Ex) Jane had to visit her **sister and** talk about her wedding. (两个动作共用一个主语，不需要使用逗号。)

当使用连词如 because、if 和 even though 时，不需要使用逗号。

Ex) Chuck could not meet his friends last **Saturday because** he had to help his brother move. (不需要使用逗号)

Ex) **Because** he had to help his brother **move**, **Chuck** could not meet his friends last **Saturday**. (需要使用逗号)

并不是所有的插入语都需要使用逗号

Ex) **The main pilot Patrick** got sick, and **the co-pilot Sam** will fly for the first time in his career.(正确，句子的主语是 Patrick 和 Sam，而名词 pilot 和 co-pilot 仅用于修饰，不需要使用逗号。)

DAY 13

PART 3 PRACTICE QUESTIONS

Choose an incorrect answer and write the correct form in the *Correction.*

1. During the Nanjing massacre, Japanese soldiers slaughtered (A) innocent Chinese, who were not (B) soldiers, depending their mood (C) of the day so that (D) one day, they decided to have a game of killing.

   ✓ *Correction:*

2. Even though (A) anyone can win the prize of 100,000 dollars by joining (B) the website, Mindy saw no point of doing so (C) because the owner of the company was a cousin, so family members would not qualify to (D) the prize.

   ✓ *Correction:*

3. The bullfrog was expanding its (A) territory with incredible rate (B) and seemed to prey for (C) anything in the way including native snakes, which were supposed to (D) be higher position in the food chain.

✓ **Correction:**

4. When the unit was engaged with (A) the conflicts (B) with the local insurgents, it could not tell who was armed (C), so the soldiers had to take extra cautions for (D) unexpected assaults.

✓ **Correction:**

5. Entering (A) the Treaty of Versailles, Germany (B) was suffering from economic depression followed by unemployment and starvation only to (C) develop its economy on the basis of (D) arms and weapons.

✓ **Correction:**

6. Indicating (A) the mistakes she made in her writing, she argued to (B) her husband to convince how necessary (C) it was for her to be completely alone in a remote place (D) when she was working.

✓ **Correction:**

7. The board members insisted about (A) making the dress code for (B) the workers, but (C) the managers kept rebutting this agenda because one more strict (D) rule could mean one fewer innovative idea.

✓ **Correction:**

8. Replacing (A) the injured participant, Jonathan joined (B) the TV survival show in the Amazon a week later (C), abiding the health department's regulation (D) for malaria injection.

✓ **Correction:**

9. Catherine <u>became so fed up of</u> (A) editing <u>spelling and grammar mistakes</u> (B) of the books in a publishing company <u>that she tried to</u> (C) change her career, but simultaneously worried about her single mother, <u>whom she had to support</u> (D).

✓ **Correction:**

10. The hard <u>truth, is that</u> (A) blockbuster <u>movies, which</u> (B) usually show huge scale <u>action and exploding scenes</u> (C), are <u>all about advertisement</u> (D).

✓ **Correction:**

11. The mountain <u>is covered of</u> (A) snow and <u>full of</u> (B) climbers <u>all year round; family climbers</u> (C) enjoy nature <u>filled with trees</u> (D) on the mid ridges and trained climbers enjoy the steep cliffs approaching the highest peak.

✓ **Correction:**

12. <u>The ex-president, Bill Clinton,</u> (A) was <u>scheduled</u> (B) to visit my school and <u>give</u> (C) a speech <u>in</u> (D) the McFerrin Hall.

✓ **Correction:**

13. The circling pattern <u>of a group ritual</u> (A) is <u>associated to</u> (B) protection from and <u>preparation for</u> (C) invasion, since each participant can carefully watch <u>the vicinity of his circling angle</u> (D).

✓ **Correction:**

14. <u>During the dynasty</u> (A), metal <u>was made to</u> (B) vessels, which <u>were soon made of</u> (C) <u>wet clay</u> (D).

✓ **Correction:**

15. Chris hated the feeling of (A) rushing to (B) all the museums and shops in the beach area, and (C) coming back to the hotel inland on the same day (D).

✓ **Correction:**

16. Invited to the party were (A) young workers from John's company, old ladies from Sally's supermarket and (B) a party band in (C) alien looking (D) costumes.

✓ **Correction:**

17. The trip to (A) the island was a serendipitous bonding experience (B) for my family for (C) the otherwise tiring, enervating (D) summer time.

✓ **Correction:**

18. When (A) Sue went out to pick (B) up the paper, there was a girl, or a young boy, (C) who (D) wanted to talk to her.

✓ **Correction:**

19. With Victor's help Jane finished eating in bed so (A) she felt (B) like owing (C) Victor a favor (D).

✓ **Correction:**

20. Having watched (A) David play (B) the harmonica, Jen was surprised. "How (C) could a guy over 70 years old have (D) such highly functioning lungs?" .

✓ **Correction:**

PART 4 ANSWERS

1. C 在 depending 后加入 on，depend on 为固定词组
2. D 把 to 改成 for
3. C 把 for 改成 on
4. A 把 with 改成 in
5. A 在 entering 后加入 into
   enter 意为进入，但是词组 enter into 意为开始做某事。
6. B 把 to 改成 with
7. A 把 about 改成 on
8. D 在 abiding 后加入 by，abide by 为固定词组
9. A 把 of 改成 with
10. A 去掉逗号
    truth 和 is 主动关系，不能用逗号连接。
11. A 把 of 改成 with
12. A 去掉逗号
    前总统有很多，所以 Bill Clinton 为关键信息，所以这里不能使用逗号。
13. B 把 to 改成 with
14. B 把 to 改成 into
    metal 是制造 vessel 的原材料，所以这里需要使用词组 made into。
15. C 去掉逗号
    当并列的两个事物共用一个主语的时候，不需要使用逗号。
16. B 在 supermarket 后使用逗号
    当列举三个或者三个以上的事物的时候，逗号需按如下标准使用：A，B，and C。
17. B 在 serendipitous 和 bonding 之间插入逗号
    当两个形容词并列出现的时候应使用 serendipitous and bonding（不用逗号），或者使用 serendipitous，bonding (不用 and)
18. C 去掉所有逗号
    当两个事物并列并用 or 连接的时候，不需要使用逗号。
19. A 加入逗号，构成 help，Jane finished eating in bed，so
    有三个不同的部分，为了表达更加清晰，每个部分之间应使用逗号分隔。
20. C 在 surprised 后插入逗号
    句子并没有结束，所以即便引用部分是一个新的句子，但它仍然是原句的一个部分，所以这里应使用逗号。

UNIT 8

DAY 14

PART 1 IDIOMS & EXPRESSIONS

PART 2 BRIEF GRAMMAR FOR IDIOMS & EXPRESSIONS

DAY 15

PART 3 PRACTICE QUESTIONS

PART 4 ANSWERS

DAY 14

PART 1 IDIOMS & EXPRESSIONS

a threat to 对……的威胁
be available for 可供……之用的
be conducive to...ing 有助于……
be equipped with 装备……
be in charge of 负责……
be in good/bad shape 处于良好 / 不好的状态
care for 喜欢，在意……
catch up with 追上 , 赶上……
deal with 处理，应付……
dispense 分配，分发
dispense with 摒弃，省略，不用……
excel in 在……方面出色
focus on 致力于，专注于……
instill in 灌输，使获得……
it is certain that... 毫无疑问
keep up with 跟上……，不落后……
notify... of 正式将（某事）通知（某人或某团体）
reply to 回复，回答
rob... of 抢夺某人的……
save time/money in 省时间 / 金钱……
take pride in 以……为骄傲
the reason (why)... is that ……的原因是……
to one’s heart’s content 让……满意的是……

PART 2 BRIEF GRAMMAR FOR IDIOMS & EXPRESSIONS

to 与其他介词的区别

如果描述的是一个动作，用 to 会更好；如果介词后接的是名词，那么尽量使用其他的介词。请看下面的范例：

Ex) Silvia went to Venice to receive the award. (正确)

Ex) Silvia went to Venice for the award. (正确)

Ex) Silvia went to Venice for receiving the award. (错误)

DAY 15

PART 3 PRACTICE QUESTIONS

Choose an incorrect answer and write the correct form in the *Correction.*

1. Since the economic situation (A) was not satisfactory (B), the new chief of the police department dispensed of (C) the formal (D) welcoming ceremony.

✓ Correction:

2. The scientists know that it (A) is necessary for creating (B) a matching equation (C) to make machine work (D) accurately.

✓ Correction:

3. Cell phones these days have been (A) equipped of (B) almost all the advanced functions (C), which traditional computers had (D).

✓ **Correction:**

4. Ted somehow feels that eating sweets (A) while working is conducive to increase (B) his work performance and, thus, has never been (C) in good shape (D).

✓ **Correction:**

5. Even though (A) the Chinese government takes a census (B) regularly, it is hard to keep up of (C) increasing rate, which (D) rapidly occurs during the census.

✓ **Correction:**

6. The thought (A) that she had to deal the angry clients (B) robbed her of sleep (C) during (D) the entire night.

✓ **Correction:**

7. When Owen saw the clothes available of (A) much less money (B) in the shop, he realized (C) that the shop was selling (D) knock off products.

✓ **Correction:**

8. It is uncertain whether (A) the judges had already decided to favor (B) the player of the host country, but certain that (C) the silver medalist performed much better than (D) did the gold medalist.

✓ **Correction:**

9. The reason Timmy does not want to take one to one lessons is because he feels unnecessary to spend money on the lessons he has no problem understanding.
A B C D

✓ Correction:

10. Countries with highly developed space technology have been preparing ways to protect the Earth from asteroids, which can be great threats of Earth.
A B C D

✓ Correction:

11. David took pride about his work, but his co-workers and supervisors were not satisfied with it and could not tell him the truth, because of his defensive nature.
A B C D

✓ Correction:

12. As a manager, Tommy notifies day and night time workers with their shifts and job details.
A B C D

✓ Correction:

13. In the first couple of days, Naomi and Kim could not resist shopping, because all the products on the streets seemed cheap and real, but after buying with their hearts' content, they realized they had paid more than they would in the duty-free shops.
A B C D

✓ Correction:

14. Kathrine is alleged to care of her children to the extreme level; she calls the school if they do not reply to her message immediately.
A B C D

✓ Correction:

15. Akim's strategy to focus over (A) high teen boys for the new cosmetics has been (B) proven sensational, and he is preparing (C) to launch another lineup for men in early twenties (D).

✓ **Correction:**

16. Terry does not like to sit and talk (A), because he does not feel in the charge of (B) a discussion in that way, so he often talks in front of (C) the group regardless of (D) the size of the events.

✓ **Correction:**

17. Great leaders not only take responsibility, but (A) instill among (B) members responsibility by showing (C) quietly but repeatedly (D) how to take responsibility.

✓ **Correction:**

18. Having retired (A) as one of the most successful basketball players (B) in the world, Michael Jordan did not excel in (C) baseball in the following years and soon decided to return (D) the basketball court.

✓ **Correction:**

19. Attempt to ignore (A) cultural differences does not save time to learn (B) a language; it (C) lengthens the time, since there are many expressions based on culture (D).

✓ **Correction:**

20. Cindy had been sick (A) for a while before the audition for the jazz orchestra and now (B) could not play as perfectly; she (C) felt the sickness had robbed her from (D) the opportunity.

PART 4 ANSWERS

1. C 把 of 改成 with
2. B 把 for creating 改成 to creat
   在关于介词 to 和 for 的选择方面，通常 to 用来引出动词，而 for 则接名词，所以在本句中，选项 B 应为 to create 或者 for。
3. B 把 of 改成 with
4. B 把 increase 改成 increasing
   词组 be conducive to 应接动名词
5. C 把 of 改成 with
6. B deal 后加入 with，固定词组 deal with
7. A 把 of 改成 for
8. A 把 whether 改成 that
   尽管在 uncertain 后使用 whether 听起来很符合逻辑，但是实际上这样会造成拖沓甚至歧义。
9. B 把 why 改成 that
   此处为固定用法，the reason why（连用）或者 the reason... is that（分开使用）。
10. D 把 of 改成 to
11. A 把 about 改成 in
12. C 把 with 改成 of
13. C 把 with 改成 to
14. B 把 of 改成 for
15. A 把 over 改成 on
16. B 去掉定冠词 the
    原词组为 be/feel in charge of
17. B 把 among 改成 in
18. D 在 return 后加入 to
    这里使用 to 表达动作的接受者
19. B 把 to learn 改成 in learning
    原词组为 save time/money in
20. D 把 from 改成 of
    原词组为 rob someone of something

UNIT 9

DAY 16

PART 1 IDIOMS & EXPRESSIONS

PART 2 BRIEF GRAMMAR FOR IDIOMS & EXPRESSIONS

DAY 17

PART 3 PRACTICE QUESTIONS

PART 4 ANSWERS

DAY 16

PART 1 IDIOMS & EXPRESSIONS

at a loss 不知所措，困惑
be fraught with 充满……
be based on 基于……
by no means 绝不，无论如何都不……
congratulate... on 就……向某人祝贺
contact = come in contact with = make contact with 联络……，与……取得联系
derive from 起源于……
fend off (ward off) 挡开……
have an intention of (intend to) 打算……
in vain 白费地，徒劳地
make sure of (to) 确定，确保
shy of 对……有顾虑；对……畏缩；缺乏
the same... as 与……同样
wreak havoc on 肆虐，对……造成巨大的破坏
zoom in/out 放大 / 缩小

PART 2 BRIEF GRAMMAR FOR IDIOMS & EXPRESSIONS

1. 关系代词 that

当作为关系代词连接两个句子的时候，that 不能使用在逗号或者任何介词之后。

Ex) Adrian bought a car, **that** did not have any warrantee. (错误，把 that 改成 which 或者去掉逗号)

Ex) Brian read the story **to that** his brother had referred. (错误，把 that 改成 which)

2. 逗号的详细用法

当句子的意图表达十分清晰的时候，使用逗号则意指逗号之间的信息属于辅助信息。

Ex) The most famous tragic story of the **ship**, **Titanic**, **has** been passed down to many generations of people.

当指代不够清晰的时候，由于限定信息的必要性，不能使用逗号。

Ex) The tragic story of the **ship Titanic has** been passed down to many generations of people.

带有逗号的分词句

当在句首或者句尾使用分词短语的时候，与主句之间使用逗号意味着分词与主句动词共享主句的主语。

Ex) Jude went to the **gym**, **wanting** to check the facility.

当主句与分词短语中间没有逗号的时候，分词短语用来修饰与其相连的名词，而不是主句的主语。

Ex) The girl group went on a **tour gathering** an astronomical number of fans. (在这个句子中，gathering 更有可能用来修饰 a tour 而不是 the girl group)

DAY 17

PART 3 PRACTICE QUESTIONS

Choose an incorrect answer and write the correct form in the *Correction*.

1. Many English words are derived by (A) other languages, such as Chinese and French, but, ironically, (B) many non-native English speakers learn the English pronunciations (C) of the words (D) again.

✓ *Correction:*

2. Vincent had a very shy and quiet quality, that many were reversely attracted to.
A B C D

✓ Correction:

3. Finding the right road was very easy. As they could find a very detailed map, which
A B C D
described each and every road in the city.

✓ Correction:

4. For the trip to Europe with Amy, Tess and Jim and his sister after the final term, Suzanne
A
prepared a schedule table so that they could make sure not to miss any important attraction.
B C D

✓ Correction:

5. Word, and grammar books are the first ones to study when students start to prepare for
A B C D
any official test.

✓ Correction:

6. To Murdock's huge success in the online game business, his friends, as well as many
A
other close, and distant family members were at a loss and did not contact him at first,
B C
even though they all wanted to be the first to congratulate him on the news.
D

✓ Correction:

7. The sales manager Lucy had all the salesmen wear suits, that they especially liked, and
A B C
go directly to the promotion site, not to the company.
D

✓ Correction:

8. After watching a movie, in which heroes fended of aliens, Jane, in vain, told Sam, who
A B C
was impressed by the movie, why she considered the movie a waste of time.
D

✓ Correction:

9. Despite (A) the great offer, Singh had to reconsider about becoming (B) an associate because (C) the company seemed fraught of (D) many obstacles to prevent efficient communication.

✓ **Correction:**

10. Before (A) the local government (B) could even estimate (C) the damage, the volcano wreaked havoc of (D) the entire city.

✓ **Correction:**

11. When Jiang decided to resume her study abroad just a couple of months shy of (A) her 40's birthday, and posted (B) the news online, many friends of hers, who were house wives, did (C) not respond; they could not understand why she chose to study (D) when she was supposed to meet a man and get married.

✓ **Correction:**

12. The movie director Steven (A) Spielberg made the famous alien movie ET, which brought (B) him international fame, but (C) other alien movies after it (D) did not have as much impact.

✓ **Correction:**

13. The movie director Steven (A) Spielberg's movie, *Catch Me if You Can*, is (B) based on (C) the life story of a real person (D).

✓ **Correction:**

14. The fast long (A) movement of tubes is (B) the best feature of the water park, even though most people feel it (C) too expensive to ride and (D) watch others enjoy them.

✓ **Correction:**

15. Zooming in the camera, Dr. Hugh by no mean had an intention of looking at the group of ladies, but of testing its functions.

A: Zooming in; B: by no mean; C: an intention of looking; D: of testing its

✓ **Correction:**

16. Children in Philippines do not have the same situation with those in other countries nearby; they are suffering not only from poverty, but also from natural disasters such as typhoon, which takes away food, houses, and loved ones.

A: in Philippines; B: the same situation with those; C: nearby; they are suffering not only from poverty; D: disasters such as typhoon, which takes away food, houses, and loved ones.

✓ **Correction:**

17. Even though some of my friends have dogs, excreting, on the streets, they don't pick up what is left by dogs and leave the scene.

A: Even though; B: dogs, excreting, on the streets; C: up; D: is left

✓ **Correction:**

18. On one summer morning, Jessica was going to work earlier than usual having a cool breeze blown in her face and listening to pop music when she saw Jack in the blue shirt in front of a bull statue.

A: On one summer morning,; B: usual having a cool breeze blown; C: listening to pop music when; D: saw Jack in the blue shirt in front of a bull statue

✓ **Correction:**

19. A series of books, called The *Lord of the Rings*, were made into movies, but many said movies were not as interesting as the books.

A: A series of books, called The *Lord of the Rings*,; B: made; C: movies, but; D: not as interesting as

✓ **Correction:**

20. The Canadian English instructor, Dennis, is responsible for all the delayed, unchecked essays, because he forgot that he would have classes today.

A: The Canadian English instructor, Dennis,; B: responsible for; C: delayed, unchecked; D: would

✓ **Correction:**

PART 4 ANSWERS

1. A 把 by 改成 from
2. B 把 that 改成 which

   that 前不能使用逗号。
3. B 把 easy 和 as 之间的句点改成逗号，As 小写为 as

   as 在这里作为连词使用，这两个分开的句子应该使用逗号连接。
4. A 插入逗号，变成 Amy，Tess，and Jim and his sister

   当列举三个或者三个以上事物的时候，逗号须按如下标准使用：A，B，and C，如果仅列举两个事物，则不需要使用逗号。
5. A 去掉逗号

   当列举两个事物并使用 and 进行连接的时候，不需要使用逗号。
6. A 改成 friends，as well as many other close and distant family members

   当使用 as well as 引导两个或者两个以上部分的时候，使用逗号；但是如果两个部分共用一个主语并使用 and 连接的时候则不需要使用逗号。
7. C 改成 suits that they especially liked and 或者 suits，which they especially liked，and

   that 前不可以使用逗号，如果想要保留 that，那么需要去掉逗号，但是如果使用 which 则可以。
8. B 把 of 改成 off
9. D 把 of 改成 with
10. D 把 of 改成 on
11. B 去掉逗号

    当两个句子用 and 连接的时候，如果这两个句子共用一个主语，则不需要使用逗号。
12. B 改成 movie，ET，brought

    史蒂芬·斯皮尔伯格的著名的外星人电影很明显是 ET，在这样的情况下，ET 不是关键信息，所以这里需要使用逗号用以表明 ET 是一个辅助性的信息。
13. B 改成 movie *Catch Me if You Can is*

因为史蒂芬•斯皮尔伯格的电影有很多，*Catch Me if You Can* 这部电影的名字对于表达句中要讨论的电影起到关键性的限定作用，所以这里去掉逗号用以提高这一信息的限定作用。

14. A 改成 The fast，long 或者 The fast and long

fast 和 long 都是形容词，所以它们是平行关系，应使用逗号或者用 and 进行连接。

15. B 把 mean 改成 means

16. B 把 with 改成 as

same...as 为固定词组

17. B 去掉逗号改成 dogs excreting on the streets

excrete 动作的发起者是 dogs，而不是 some of my friends；另外，on the streets 前也不需要使用逗号。

18. B 改成 usual，having a cool breeze blown

going to work，having a cool breeze 和 listening to pop music 共用同一个主语 Jessica，因此应使用逗号连接。

19. A 改成 the series of books called *The Lord of the Rings*

我们并不知道书的名字，所以 The Lord of the Rings 在句中是关键信息，需要去掉逗号。

20. A 去掉逗号，改成 The Canadian English instructor Dennis

我们不能知道 instructor 的名字，所以 Dennis 在句中是关键信息，因此不需要使用逗号。

UNIT 10

DAY 18

PART 1 IDIOMS & EXPRESSIONS

PART 2 BRIEF GRAMMAR FOR IDIOMS & EXPRESSIONS

DAY 19

PART 3 PRACTICE QUESTIONS

PART 4 ANSWERS

DAY 18

PART 1 IDIOMS & EXPRESSIONS

a critic of ……的评论家
adhere to 遵循，依附
appeal to 向……投诉；向……呼吁；对……有吸引力
be acquainted with 对……熟悉
be convinced of 确信，认识到，对……深信不疑
be comparable to(with) 与……可比较的，比得上……的
be devoid of 缺乏……
be distinct from 与……有区别
be jealous of 妒忌
be married to 与……结婚
be made up of 由……组成
be susceptible to 易受……影响的；易为……左右的
be unique to 是……独有的，特有的
be worth... ing/noun 值得……
be worthy of... ing/noun 配得上，对得起，当之无愧
by accident 偶然地
by design 故意地，蓄意地
by mistake 错误地
catch sight of 看见……
collaborate with someone in...ing/noun 与……进行合作
come down with 染上，得了 (病)
come to a conclusion 得出结论
come to terms with 与……达成协议
cooperate with 与……合作
cope with 处理，应付
enable... to 使……能够……

encourage... to 鼓励……
endow A with B 把 B 捐赠给 A
discourage... from 阻止……
fill out 填写（表格等）……
have a resemblance to 与……相似
in addition to...ing 除了……之外，还
in recognition of 承认……而……，为酬答……而……
in response to (respond to) 对……做出反应
in regard to 关于……
in search of 寻找……
insulate against 防止……，与……隔绝
knock over 碰翻 , 轻易击败
make sense of 搞清……的意思
of a descent 有……的血统
on account of 由于，基于
on display 展出
on the brink of 濒于……
prior to 在……之前
stock-in-trade 存货，现货
stop by 顺便拜访，顺路探望
suspect... of (be suspicious of) 怀疑
relate to 涉及，与……有关系
remind... of 提醒……
respond to 对……做出反应
wear out (使) 磨损；(使) 用坏
work in profession 工作

PART 2 BRIEF GRAMMAR FOR IDIOMS & EXPRESSIONS

1. Resemble

resemble 必须单独使用，不能与任何介词连用。

Ex) Timothy **was resembled with** his uncle.

(错误，不能用被动语态，也不能与任何介词连用)

Ex) Timothy resembles his uncle. (正确)

DAY 19

PART 3 PRACTICE QUESTIONS

Choose an incorrect answer and write the correct form in the *Correction.*

1. Filling out (A) the investigation forms with stock-of-trade (B) stories that could happen in every operation, Dan was now afraid that his partner Sid would not (C) cooperate with the stories (D).

✓ **Correction:**

2. Last spring (A) the South Korean government combined (B) three official bodies regarding disaster and rescue (C) in response with (D) the dropping support for the government.

✓ **Correction:**

3. Though Ray was very nice when (A) he was with the rest of the platoon, as a trainer for snipers (B), he did not give (C) any face to which (D) he was acquainted any break during the training session.

✓ **Correction:**

4. When Curt was introduced to (A) Jeff's fiancé, he (B) could not help feeling jealousy (C) of Jeff by the young look (D) of the fiancé.

✓ **Correction:**

5. Sami's dog always (A) runs away at the sight of (B) a cat, a weird behavior (C) unique with (D) her dog.

✓ **Correction:**

6. The hospital administrators collected money for Kenneth, enabling (A) him to receive a heart transplant operation; this (B) reminded many people in the hospital, such as doctors, nurses, and patients, of the movie *John Q* (C), which resembled with (D) Kenneth's situation.

✓ **Correction:**

7. Mindy knocked over (A) the iron by mistake (B), but only burned the surface of her left sock, one of the pair which (C) she had bought to insulate her feet for (D) cold.

✓ **Correction:**

8. Johnson stopped by (A) Jane's apartment and saw henry's bag in the study by the accident (B), but did not ask if she invited him by design (C) to show there was something going on between her (D) and Henry.

✓ **Correction:**

9. Although (A) Dillon went to India for the search of (B) opportunity, he had never expected (C) to meet and get married to (D) an Indian woman, who would enable him to succeed internationally.

✓ **Correction:**

10. Individuals who (A) work for (B) professions that have enormous interactions with other people tend to (C) have higher stress rate and remain quiet after work (D).

✓ **Correction:**

11. Randall is a critic about (A) the current space technology; he believes that more investment on the space travel (B) will make the technology develop (C) faster as more people are interested in (D) entertainment.

✓ **Correction:**

12. Devoid of (A) a true successor from (B) Hui descent, the members of Hui reserve project were getting worn out (C) when the chairman decided to tell the congressman that the project would (D) be delayed.

✓ **Correction:**

13. At the first sight I could make sense of (B) the painting because it (C) was barely distinct with (D) other paintings of the artist.

✓ **Correction:**

14. Some of Korean soap operas' appeal with (A) an astronomical number of (B) viewers in Asia is comparable to (C) or bigger than that of (D) Hollywood stars in the same region.

✓ **Correction:**

15. In addition to invite (A) Ricardo's relatives from Argentina, Anya considers having (B) the wedding again in Argentina since their marriage (C) is international (D).

✓ **Correction:**

16. In recognition for (A) James' extraordinary ability to (B) write songs, Cindy called his manager, wishing (C) to collaborate with (D) James.

✓ **Correction:**

17. Mr. Jonathan did not like to fix Lucy's essays as deeply (A) as other students' (B) essays on account about (C) her pride (D).

✓ **Correction:**

18. Although (A) the Japanese government and many organizations regarding (B) human rights pled, the Singapore government detained the two Japanese, (C) who were suspected to be (D) drug traffickers.

✓ **Correction:**

19. The local government do not encourage expatriates responding (A) to unfair and unjust scenes among (B) the local people; in fact, they are discouraged from (C) engaging in any kind of (D) dispute with the local people.

✓ **Correction:**

20. Most of (A) the residents in the island are convinced for (B) the significance of the policy relating to (C) the fish quota (D).

✓ **Correction:**

PART 4 ANSWERS

1. B 把 of 改成 in
2. D 把 with 改成 to
3. D 把 to which 改成 with which

   be acquainted with 是固定词组，此为非限定性定语从句介词提前。
4. C 把 jealousy 改成 jealous

   jealousy 是名词，放在 feel 后的应为形容词，故做如上修改。
5. D 把 with 改成 to
6. D 去掉 with

   resemble 为及物动词，不需要使用介词。
7. D 把 for 改成 against
8. B 去掉 the
9. B 把 for the 改成 in
10. B 把 for 改成 in
11. A 把 about 改成 of
12. B 把 from 改成 of
13. D 把 with 改成 from
14. A 把 with 改成 to
15. A 把 invite 改成 inviting

    词组 in addition to 后应接名词或动名词。
16. A 把 for 改成 of
17. C 把 about 改成 of
18. D 把 to be 改成 of being
19. A 把 responding 改成 to respond

    原词组为 encourage someone to do something
20. B 把 for 改成 of

UNIT 11

DAY 20

PART 1 IDIOMS & EXPRESSIONS

PART 2 BRIEF GRAMMAR FOR IDIOMS & EXPRESSIONS

PART 3 PRACTICE QUESTIONS

PART 4 ANSWERS

DAY 20

PART 1 IDIOMS & EXPRESSIONS

adjust to 调整，调节
attest to 证实……
be attuned to 调节，习惯于
be synonymous with 等同于
be talented at 在……方面有天赋
between... and... 在……与……之间
can (can't) afford to 能（不能）买得起（当使用 to 时，应接动词原形）
can (can't) afford + a noun 能（不能）买得起
catch someone off guard 使某人措手不及
commit... to... ing 致力于……
dedicate... to... ing/noun 致力于……
devote... to... ing/noun 致力于……
impact on 在……上的影响
in tandem (with) 与……同时发生
interfere with 妨碍，干扰
intervene in 干涉，介入
keep pace with 并驾齐驱，赶上，跟上
limit... to... 使……受……的限制
make room for 给……让出地方
not so much A as B 与其说 A 不如说 B
offer of 提供（物）；给予（物）；提议
take place 发生
take the place of 代替，替换
tend to (have a tendency to) 倾向于……

PART 2 BRIEF GRAMMAR FOR IDIOMS & EXPRESSIONS

limit

limit 是一个用来限定意图、行为、想法、安排等的名词。

Ex) The spending limit of her credit card was extended last month.

但是当 limit 用作动词与 to 或者 from 连用的时候，意思就稍有不同了。

Ex) My cat limits herself to the living room. (我的猫只住在客厅里。)

Ex) My cat limits herself from the living room. (我的猫从来不进客厅。)

PART 3 PRACTICE QUESTIONS

Choose an incorrect answer and write the correct form in the *Correction.*

1. When Rosie moved to the city, she had to adjust with (A) many cases; she neither knew (B) how to take a cab nor (C) understood (D) how to use the subway.

✓ *Correction:*

2. Lindsay does not like teachers who interfere (A) reading practice by explaining the definition of words; she believes that it (B) is more important to catch the meaning of the whole passage, and (C) there should be no interruption on the way (D).

✓ *Correction:*

3. The marshal intervened in (A) the gang related (B) conflict in the area with (C) the offer for (D) a peaceful negotiation.

✓ *Correction:*

4. When Wendy decided to attend the school, she was sure that she would commit her entire time to develop her talent as an artist, but soon lost interest and wanted to transfer again.
(A: attend the school; B: to develop; C: as an artist; D: lost interest)

✓ **Correction:**

5. Managers blamed workers; workers, poor display; board members, mismanagement for the decline of customers, but the CEO June thought that all of these factors had been working with tandem.
(A: workers, poor display; board members, mismanagement; B: the CEO June; C: had been; D: with tandem)

✓ **Correction:**

6. Many stories of Greek myth have been accepted by some of contemporary historians because scientists and historians cannot attest the stance that the stories never happened.
(A: have been accepted; B: contemporary; C: attest the stance; D: never happened)

✓ **Correction:**

7. While Jack and Wendy were talking about their wedding plan, he was caught of off guard and frustrated by her question about the plan for a new car.
(A: were talking; B: he; C: caught of off guard; D: frustrated by)

✓ **Correction:**

8. The disastrous accident of the ship Titanic had a significant impact not only about ship building and safety regulations, but also on movie and book productions.
(A: the ship Titanic; B: not only about; C: building and safety; D: but also on movie)

✓ **Correction:**

9. Nina hated Jason not so much for his deceptive nature yet for his surprisingly skilled business ability.
(A: hated; B: deceptive; C: yet; D: surprisingly)

✓ **Correction:**

10. Rene's cat Oscar (A) is not tractable and has Rene devote (B) her full attention to take (C) care of him; otherwise (D) he excretes everywhere in the house.

✓ **Correction:**

11. Although (A) Chen tried to be fair for her team members, she (B) couldn't afford taking (C) everyone to the conference (D) in the Bahamas.

✓ **Correction:**

12. Putting the frosting between the nose to (A) the mouth of the face shaped cake destroyed by handling (B) too carelessly was (C) Lucy, the baker and mother of the one year old boy, whom (D) she made the cake for.

✓ **Correction:**

13. Matt has a tendency for exaggerating (A) what he hears (B) and to change (C) the protagonist of the story as if he experienced (D) everything.

✓ **Correction:**

14. Billy, my cousin's dog, (A) is attuned for the life (B) in the wild; it sleeps well under a tree and is very sensitive to (C) the slight movement in the surroundings (D).

✓ **Correction:**

15. The reason the criminal dedicated so much on taking (A) care of (B) poor people was that (C) he could (D) find a possible target.

✓ **Correction:**

16. Many students find it surprising (A) that so many words are synonymous to (B) the words in the question parts that (C) they need to figure out (D) the sentence structure.

✓ **Correction:**

17. Even though blind (A), Sean can keep a pace with (B) or be better (C) than other swimmers because of (D) the sensors in his ears and the cap.

✓ **Correction:**

18. Having moved (A) to a small apartment, Henry has been struggling (B) to make a room for (C) the treehouse for his cat, which (D) does not sleep and cries during the night without it.

✓ **Correction:**

19. Shawn will take place of (A) the two managers of (B) the old companies when (C) the merger takes place (D).

✓ **Correction:**

20. Students, who are talented at (A) sports, should not (B) limit themselves only for (C) physical development; in order to succeed in the professional sports world, they (D) need to be also good at academic subjects.

✓ **Correction:**

PART 4 ANSWERS

1. A 把 with 改成 to
2. A 在 interfere 后加入 with
3. D 把 for 改成 of
   of 这里用来解释 peaceful negotiation，而 for 则用以表达目的。
4. B 把 to develop 改成 to developing
   词组 commit to 后应使用名词或动名词。
5. D 把 with 改成 in
6. C 改成 在 attest 后加 to，此为固定词组
7. C 去掉 of，改成 caught off guard
8. B 把 about 改成 on
9. C 把 yet 改成 as
   not so much as 为固定词组。
10. C 把 to take 改成 to taking
    词组 devote to 后应接名词或动名词。
11. C 把 taking 改成 to take
12. A 把 to 改成 and
    between 和 and 为固定搭配。
13. A 把 for exaggerating 改成 to exaggerate
    have a tendency to 是正确的。
14. B 把 for 改成 to
15. A 把 on taking 改成 to taking
    词组 dedicate to 后应接名词或动名词。
16. B 把 to 改成 with
17. B 去掉不定冠词 a，构成词组 keep pace with
18. C 去掉不定冠词 a，构成词组 make room for
19. A 插入定冠词 the
    take place 意为发生，为了表达 Shawn 将要接任这一职务的意思，这里需要使用 take the place。
20. C 把 for 改成 to
    句子意为它们不应该只关注身体发展，所以 limit to 更加合适。

UNIT 12

DAY 21

PART 1 IDIOMS & EXPRESSIONS

PART 2 PRACTICE QUESTIONS

PART 3 ANSWERS

DAY 21

PART 1 IDIOMS & EXPRESSIONS

adapt to 变得习惯于……，使适应……
A is to B as(what) C is to D A 和 B 的关系就像 C 和 D 的关系那样
agree on 双方或多方在某件事情上取得一致
(a) means of ……的方法
be exposed to 暴露于……之下
be far away from 远离……
be far from (never) 远非……
belong to 属于……
be prone to 易于……的
be tolerable to (intolerable to) 对……可以（不可以）容忍
compensate for 为……做出补偿
conjure up 使……浮现于脑海，使联想到
consistent with (inconsistent with) 与……一致（不一致）
emerge from 从……中浮现，出现
for fear of (for fear that) 以免，为了避免……
gain(get) an edge over(on) 对……获得优势，胜过……
indulge in 沉溺于……
in the presence of 在……面前
make a living 赚钱生活
name after 以……的名字命名
passion for 对……的激情，爱好
protest against 抗议……
react to 对……做出反应
succeed in 在……中取得成功
succeed to 继承，继任
take notice of 注意到……
to one's hesrt's content 尽情地，心满意足地

PART 2 PRACTICE QUESTIONS

Choose an incorrect answer and write the correct form in the *Correction.*

1. People in the third world are proner to (A) diseases related to (B) the dirty environment, and so their life expectancy is shorter (C) than that of those who (D) live in the developed countries.

✓ Correction:

2. Most of language instructors in ESL program agree (A) that students need to succeed to apply (B) simple and easy sentences, since English works in harmony (C), not in each and individual sentence (D).

✓ Correction:

3. When Jimmy gets intractable (A) and disciplined at school (B), he often makes an excuse (C) that his father will succeed him to the business (D).

✓ Correction:

4. Unlike what many believe, the kiwi fruit is native in China (A), but named after the kiwi bird (B) in New Zealand; because (C) most of the kiwi fruit consumed in the world is produced in New Zealand, it was commercially beneficial (D) for New Zealand to call it Kiwi when it started to be produced in New Zealand.

✓ Correction:

5. That students who (A) are exposed with the smells (B) from snacks in the classroom will not be able to concentrate on (C) the lesson is why Tim does not agree on (D) school's plan.

✓ Correction:

6. The defense department decided not to (A) install the stealth function on the fighters (B) because it (C) found out that the radar systems could still react with (D) the fighters with the function.

✓ **Correction:**

7. Even though (A) Sammy had lived (B) in China for eight years, he was far away from (C) adapting himself to (D) the real Chinese culture when his sister visited him, because he had hardly learned the Chinese language or met the local people.

✓ **Correction:**

8. When Ms. Michelle wanted to confirm if John would come to participate in (A) the presentation the next day, he was hesitating to give an answer, so (B) she could know he was inconsistent about (C) his earlier statement in the presence of (D) his parents.

✓ **Correction:**

9. Having quit (A) the job, Jason established his own (B) shop that was intolerable with (C) the owners of his previous shop because (D) the two shops were very close.

✓ **Correction:**

10. Full House, the title of (A) the TV talk show, may conjure the poker game (B), but the show is about (C) the relationships among (D) the family members of various celebrities.

✓ **Correction:**

11. Those who indulge on (A) the role playing computer games can show paranoia and lack the passion for (B) work and study because (C) the virtual world can compensate for (D) what they cannot achieve in reality.

✓ **Correction:**

12. With (A) a minor infection in (B) the eyes, Kirill enjoyed the party with his heart's content (C), but the next morning when he woke up, he found out that the infection had gotten worse (D).

✓ *Correction:*

13. When (A) Linda walked out of (B) the airport security area, she took a notice of (C) many photographers and reporters, who had been waiting (D) to ask her about the scandal.

✓ *Correction:*

14. That (A) rice is to Japanese for (B) wheat is to American does not (C) apply for Chinese because the preferred food differs from (D) region to region.

✓ *Correction:*

15. His day job was a mean of (A) sustaining his family, but (B) the short stories he wrote (C) after work were a way to realize his dream (D).

✓ *Correction:*

16. Ellen strongly protested on (A) the school's policy to keep the students at school after classes (B) and have them finish (C) homework if they did not do (D) it.

✓ *Correction:*

17. Most people work most of days to make living (A), but they don't know they can be successful (B) if they find a goal and focus on (C) it even though they don't earn anything in the beginning (D).

✓ *Correction:*

18. Mikhail, for fear to get (A) blamed and fired, called his supervisor first and (B) explained why (C) the customers put negative remarks on (D) Yelp website.

✓ **Correction:**

19. Neither the car nor (A) the bike belongs (B) Henry; he uses public transportations and does not (C) have to worry about (D) alcohol intake during the party.

✓ **Correction:**

20. The countries which quickly emerged from (A) feudalism were industrialized before (B) other countries nearby, gaining (C) an edge above them (D).

✓ **Correction:**

PART 3 ANSWERS

1. A 把 proner 改成 more prone

   prone 的比较级和最高级分别为 more/the most prone。

2. B 把 to apply 改成 in applying

   succeed to 意为继续，与句子本意不符，因此做如上修改。

3. D 把 his father will succeed him to the business 改成 he will succeed to his father's business

   词组 succeed to 的正确使用顺序为 someone succeed to something，这里的 someone 是将来会继续做这件事的人。

4. A 把 in 改成 to
5. B 把 with 改成 to
6. D 把 with 改成 to
7. C 去掉 away，构成词组 far from。

   far from 意为远不是，而 far away from 则意为很远。

8. C 把 about 改成 with
9. C 把 with 改成 to
10. B 加入 up，构成词组 conjure up。
11. A 把 on 改成 in
12. C 把 with 改成 to，构成词组 to one's heart's content。
13. C 去掉不定冠词 a，构成词组 take notice of。
14. B 把 for 改成 as（what）
15. A 把 mean 改成 means

    虽然 means 看起来像是个复数，当意为方法或途径的时候，means 实际上是另外一个名词，而这种情况下 a means 或者 means 都是正确的。

16. A 把 on 改成 against
17. A 插入不定冠词 a，构成词组 make a living。
18. A 把 to get 改成 of getting
19. B 在 belongs 后插入 to
20. D 把 above 改成 over

REAL TESTS

REAL TEST 1

1. Before the local government could even estimate the damage, the volcano wreaked havoc
A B C D
for the entire city. No error
E

2. The corrupted bodies were observed by him as they succeeded to the source of life. No error
A B C D E

3. What she told us about his behavior differed from his claim that he was very generously
A B C
towards his family. No error
D E

4. Dr. Yamaha could not help but laugh at the sight of Steve; he would have walked around
A B C
the campus with the graffiti on the forehead. No error
D E

5. The Canadian English instructor Chris is responsible about all the delayed, unchecked
A B C
essays, because he forgot that he would have classes today. No error
D E

6. When Wendy decided to attend the school, she was sure that she committed her entire
A B
time to developing her talent as an artist, but soon lost interest and wanted to transfer
C D
again. No error
E

7. Neither John alone nor the whole members was responsible for the collaborating work
A B C
between the two schools, which was not done by deadline. No error
D E

8. Kevin finally finished singing after trying more than two hours and making the whole
A B C
cameramen exhausted. No error
D E

9. Happiness is not equivalent with money; happiness cannot be made while money can be
A B C
achieved. No error
D E

10. One of the benefits to the area is that the residents use only a small stretch of land so that
A B C
many plots are left emptied for development. No error
D E

11. The frogs are most like to survive the rainy season, and after the season their population
A B C
will unstoppably increase. No error
D E

12. Widespread snow followed by strong wind can result avalanches, which have dangerous
A B C
effects on the skiers. No error
D E

13. When you mortgage your home, you should be aware of the terms the bank puts forth.
A B C D
No error
E

14. Contrary with the praises that the futuristic novel, 2001: A space odyssey, delved into
A
religious and philosophical aspects of fear and anxiety, Stephen does not like the book
B C
because the ending part seems to him just an easy way to end the story the author could
D
not handle. No error
E

15. When living in a dense packed residential area, one should refrain from playing loud music.
A B C D
No error
E

16. Curtis, a Canadian teacher, who has spent two years in China, is well known due to his
A B C D
funny teaching skills. No error
E

17. The number of students who know the deadline of the Physics homework is very small.
A B C D
No error
E

18. Lisa hates to watch horror movies because she cannot escape thinking of the scenes in
A B C
the movies. No error
D E

19. A number of students, even though they know the deadline of Physics homework, insists
A B C
that the professor did not say it clearly. No error
D E

20. People are obsessed with success, which seems unreachable; every time they feel
A B
accomplished, they soon acknowledge that bigger success awaits us. No error
C D E

21. She is longing (A) for buy (B) a new skirt, since (C) it is getting warm (D). No error (E)

22. When Jerry watched his food rapidly grinding in (A) with Rosie's (B), he suddenly burst (C) into tears (D). No error (E)

23. The bullfrog was expanding their (A) territory with incredible rate (B) and seemed to prey on (C) anything in the way including native snakes, which were supposed to (D) be higher position in the food chain. No error (E)

24. Drivers should be careful (A) not to use the brake often on (B) a road covered with snow (C) because cars have a tendency of slipping (D) when they hit the brake. No error (E)

25. The spraying (A) paint changed the color of (B) the wall to (C) green instead from blue. (D) No error (E)

26. A couple of months ago, (A) she has said (B) she was done with (C) dating the senior, but I saw them (D) in the cinema yesterday. No error (E)

27. Since (A) the sight of (B) the beggar she saw (C) yesterday, Elizabeth feels a pang of guilt (D). No error (E)

28. Not until June saw (A) an ophthalmologist, who (B) said his eye problem was not infectious, he told (C) his co-workers in regard to (D) his red eyes. No error (E)

29. Kim referred about (A) many expressions (B) when she was working on (C) her term paper on the 18th century (D) English literature. No error (E)

30. Randall is a critic of (A) the current space technology; he believes that more investment on the space travel (B) will make the technology to develop (C) faster as more people are interested in (D) entertainment. No error (E)

REAL TEST 2

1. Harry wanted to reject to participate in the talent show, but his sister insisted that he
A B
perform and make her happy. No error
C D E

2. When you are stang by a wild bee, you should identify which bee is responsible for the
A B C
wound in case of an allergy reaction. No error
D E

3. Most parents believe that smart phones are not harmful to their children, being helpful
A B C
for brain activity. No error
D E

4. Most nocturnal animals hide themselves during the day and search food during the night.
A B C D
No error
E

5. China has the most advanced technology in hand in the space field, which need to be
A B C
tested more. No error
D E

6. Teachers can help a new student acclimate to studying well in the new school
A B C
environment by active introducing other students. No error
D E

7. The effects of exercise are not only shown in the person's movement; clear in our
A B C D
appearance. No error
E

8. Drivers in the F1, a type of racing concerned of speed racing, should be interested in
A B C
simulated racing games. No error
D E

9. It suddenly rained a lot, which flooded the whole paddy, but farmers suffered through the
A B C
bigger flood from the typhoon in the following month. No error
D E

10. Susan asked her brother, Sam, (A) if he was willing (B) to partake in (C) the talent show at school (D). No error (E)

11. I don't understand (A) why Mr. Jim opposes to (B) the legislation, which (C) his party has eagerly (D) supported. No error (E)

12. Experts likened the defeat of the Russian soccer team, a predecessor (A) of the Russian woman soccer team notorious for (B) the loose organization, to (C) Canadian soccer team (D). No error (E)

13. When Owen saw the clothes available with (A) much less money (B) in the shop, he realized (C) that the shop was selling (D) knockout products. No error (E)

14. Even after the long and arduous (A) treatment, people, if known to be (B) compulsive gamblers, can not resist to ruin (C) their life by playing card games (D). No error (E)

15. Daisy has just started practicing (A) after the long break from an injury (B), but many hurdles (C) seem to be in her way (D). No error (E)

16. The house renovation would have finished (A) a month ago, but put on hold (B) during the short rainy season, which lasted (C) longer and caused serious problems on the roof (D). No error (E)

17. It is not until (A) he met her that (B) Jay had any chance (C) of success (D). No error (E)

18. Although worried of (A) not coming back (B) on time to work on Monday, Pam planned for (C) the trip to Central America (D). No error (E)

19. By virtue of (A) his intelligence and charm (B), Alex could successfully (C) become captain (D) of the debating club. No error (E)

20. It has long been believed (A) that the last comma at the end (B) of a series of (C) words should be put when the grammar rules came into existence (D) in modern British dictionaries. No error (E)

21. Having been slow (A) to comprehend his brother's preoccupation in (B) learning German, Joshua was surprised to hear (C) that his family might have to (D) move to Germany. No error (E)

22. Having waited for an hour, Chris pretended as indifferent to Tom, since he could look
A B C
vulnerable by showing anger. No error
D E

23. In the beginning of the war, the Japanese army was superior not only in weapons; also in
A B
tactics better than those of other countries in the region. No error
C D E

24. No sooner had Rachel joined the new agency to prepare for international competition,
A B C
her old agency sued her for breaking the contract. No error
D E

25. The way she treats people makes everyone in the conference ill in ease. No error
A B C D E

26. Clayton's warm smile and sense of humor put his students at easiness during the class
A B
that he can approach each problem very closely. No error
C D E

27. Despite of the innate physical disadvantages, Henry won many international competitions.
A B C D
No error
E

28. The board members insisted in making the dress code for the workers, but the managers
A B C
kept rebutting this agenda because one more strict rule could mean one fewer innovative
D
idea. No error
E

29. John is regarded as passionately preoccupied with learning Tango and tries to participate
A B C D
in as many dancing contests. No error
E

30. My mother's zeal support in favor of longer school hours has often engaged family
A B
members with the heated discussion. No error
C D E

REAL TEST 3

1. Young children can develop their motor and perceptual skills with hand-on hobbies. No error
   A B C D E

2. The last resort to rid his cat from fleas is to shave completely, but nobody in the pet shop
   A B C
   wants to hold the cat. No error
   D E

3. The documentary film about the Amazon forests was not accessible to many viewers,
   A B C
   who were not concerned of the environment. No error
   D E

4. Managers in the company objected to the new working hour policy, because they were
   A B
   used to leave work at six and did not want to stay longer. No error
   C D E

5. The boy band consists 6 members, who are under the age of 16, and has a broad fan base.
   A B C D
   No error
   E

6. The workers in the construction site is often involved in physical confrontations because
   A B
   they are provided by three competing companies. No error
   C D E

7. The paper by John's group did not take into account the prisoner's dilemma instead they
   A B C
   dealt with the social structure of orangutans. No error
   D E

8. The movie was not acceptable for many Israelis, who found some scenes very offensive
   A B
   in dealing with historical background of their country and religion. No error
   C D E

9. Mindy knocked over the iron by mistake, but it only burned the surface of her left sock,
   A
   one of the pair which she bought to insulate her feet against cold. No error
   B C D E

10. The recent expedition of the space probe sent many beautiful pictures of landscapes of
    A B
    the other planets that comprise the solar system. No error
    C D E

11. Despite being (A) outgoing, Daisy (B) has difficulty making a friend (C) with Dr. Hammel because of his shyness (D). No error (E)

12. Hanna is capable to persuade (A) in a very hard position; she was able to (B) make her mother support (C) her after failing (D) the same business twice. No error (E)

13. Nick suggested returning (A) Gorge the smart phone, but (B) I did not see the point of it unless (C) she first promised to pay for (D) the fee. No error (E)

14. Jen was not negligent of (A) cleaning her dorm room, but (B) she was rather disorganized that after putting away (C) her stuff from the couch, the room looked as clean as any normal girl (D). No error (E)

15. Ray was not capable of (A) paying for his debt (B) back to his friends, who (C) had no choice but calling (D) his father. No error (E)

16. The success of her school is attributed (A) in part because of Adam (B), the math teacher, who (C) contributed to increasing (D) the reputation. No error (E)

17. To her surprise (A), Mike, who had never taken (B) care of house choirs, voluntarily said he would look at (C) why TV was not working (D). No error (E)

18. Trees that live in polluted areas are contact with (A) a large numbers (B) of harmful heavy metals in the ground, because most of them feed on (C) nutrients from the soil (D). No error (E)

19. People in the third world are more prone to (A) diseases related to (B) the dirty environment, and so their life expectancy is shorter (C) than those who (D) live in the developed countries. No error (E)

20. Lisa was fond of looking to (A) the dictionary even when (B) she was pretty sure of (C) the accuracy of words and sentences (D). No error (E)

21. Before the final term (A), Sam and Tim had determined (B) to study, but as a result of (C) the football game and the party afterward, he (D) received rather disappointing grades. No error (E)

22. Lou got furious at the news that Sunny, second in command, had postponed to visit the
A B C
car factory without telling him anything. No error
D E

23. Pagers were quickly giving their way to cell-phones at the end of 1990s and now are used
A B C
mostly by doctors and criminals. No error
D E

24. The metal sculpture was made mainly of iron, and thus we cannot display them outside
A B C
because of the possibility of becoming rusty. No error
D E

25. Zack wrote the letter of plea in vain because he had got caught red-handedly and the
A B C
police would not give him any break. No error
D E

26. When I went to the airport to see her about, I came across a group of Japanese tourists,
A B
who had no idea of where to catch a cab. No error
C D E

27. Denny, who has just graduated, as well as his brothers, who have many years of
A B
experience in the field of chemical engineering, has come to the conclusion that working
C D
in the same company should not be the best option. No error
E

28. As I was familiar to the painting, the painter was also familiar to me. No error
A B C D E

29. Thanks to Julie's sister, we could have entered the test center in time and have some time
A B C
to calm down before the test. No error
D E

30. Just as the other Asian teams, such as Iranian and Japanese soccer team, lost all the
A
matches in the first round in the world cup, also Korean team was eliminated in the first
B C D
round. No error
E

REAL TEST 4

1. Clara was more satisfied with (A) her son's decision than his choice of major, because (B) she had been worried that he would (C) be very indefinite (D) about the future. No error (E)

2. At large (A) for more than three days, the deserter has been believed (B) to hide in one of the mountains around (C) his army camp or crossed (D) the border line. No error (E)

3. When Jimmy gets intractable (A) and disciplined at school (B), he often makes an excuse (C) that he will succeed (D) his father's business. No error (E)

4. The movie was worth watching (A); plots, characters and (B) visual and sound (C) effects were all above (D) my expectation. No error (E)

5. Suzie was certain for (A) getting an A (B) in history, because she handed in (C) an extra paper for additional reading (D). No error (E)

6. Professor Hue does not hand out (A) homework often (B), and this is the biggest reason (C) his lectures are often full (D). No error (E)

7. Even though (A) he looked very suspiciously (B), the detectives could not continue anymore, and decided (C) to get the warrant to search (D) his house. No error (E)

8. Finding Japanese similar to (A) his native language, Zhang changed his mind and decided studying (B) English first, since he believed accomplishing (C) something more difficult would save him more time for (D) something easier like Japanese. No error (E)

9. Joana and her fiancé are meeting with their parents from both sides (A) to discuss (B) financial issues for their marriage, such as how the house should be big (C) and what kind of furniture (D)

it should have. No error
E

10. By order of the chief of police department of New York, the chaos, which seemed
A B
impossible to control, was fastly and effectively getting under control. No error
C D E

11. Most citizens are now oblivious to the accident, which took away over 200 lives, but the
A
radio station has still been keeping up with the news of it every morning. No error
B C D E

12. Most expatriates in pursuit of jobs outside their own countries should prove that he or she
A B
has bachelor degrees and no history of criminal activity. No error
C D E

13. Even though Jose zealously endeavors to supplant the corn based oil with fish based one,
A
the investment for the study is likely to be called out, and he will have to put off the study
B C D
until he finds another investor. No error
E

14. The war dispossessed the young generation of hopes and wishes for their future and families.
A B C D
No error
E

15. Negative effects of consuming excessive sugar have been greatly emphasized, but modern
A B
people are actually in need of paying attention in consuming excessive salt to keep healthier
C D
body. No error
E

16. The bad conditions of the football players are most likely to ascribe to jet lag. No error
A B C D E

17. During the Nanjing massacre, Japanese soldiers slaughtered innocent Chinese people,
A
who were not soldiers, depending on their mood of the day so that one day, they decided
B C D
to have a game of killing. No error
E

18. Even though anyone could win the prize of 100,000 dollars by joining the website,
A B
my sister saw no point of it because the owner of the company was a cousin, so family
C
members would not qualify for the prize. No error
D E

19. Because of the innocent nature, Carrie has a hard time even to talk to someone accused
A B C D
of lying. No error
E

20. When the unit was engaged of (A) the conflicts with (B) the local insurgents, it could not tell who was armed (C), so the soldiers had to take extra cautions for (D) unexpected assaults. No error (E)

21. After watching a movie, in which heroes warded off (A) aliens, Jane in vain (B) talked to Sam, who was very impressed by it (C), why she considered the movie a waste of time (D). No error (E)

22. Entering into (A) the Treaty of Versailles, Germany was suffering (B) economic depression followed by unemployment and starvation only to (C) develop its economy on the basis of arms and weapons (D). No error (E)

23. Although (A) Jim needed to have (B) his computer fixed (C), he kept using (D) it until he made enough money to buy a new one. No error (E)

24. In addition to inviting (A) Ricardo's relatives from Argentina, Anya considers to have (B) the wedding again in Argentina since their marriage (C) is international (D). No error (E)

25. His friends could not find any method of stopping (A) water from back (B) rushing, so (C) Harrison had to call the plumber and paid even more than he had anticipated (D). No error (E)

26. When she arrived at the meeting, most agendas had been (A) already dealt with (B), but the rest of the board members (C) still wanted her to account about (D) some of the agendas. No error (E)

27. Replacing (A) the injured participant, Jonathan joined (B) the TV survival show in the Amazon a week later (C), abiding by (D) the health department's regulation for malaria injection. No error (E)

28. Akim's strategy to focus on (A) high teen boys for the new cosmetics have been (B) proven sensational, and he is preparing (C) to launch another lineup for men in early twenties (D). No error (E)

29. Gerry's parents were looking (A) forward to seeing (B) the math teacher, who did not look at (C) his potential weaknesses (D). No error (E)

30. Terry does not like to sit and talk (A), because he does not feel in charge of (B) a discussion in that way, so he often talks in front of (C) the group regardless (D) the size of the events. No error (E)

REAL TEST 5

1. Great leaders not only take responsibility, but instill in members responsibility by showing quietly but repeatedly how to take responsibility in the members' mistakes. No error
(A: but; B: in; C: by showing; D: in; E: No error)

2. Having retired as one of the most successful basketball players in the world, Michael Jordan did not excel in baseball in the following years and soon decided returning to the basketball court. No error
(A: Having retired; B: the most successful basketball players; C: excel in; D: returning to; E: No error)

3. Kim does not adjust herself well to the new environment, and in fact her mother has had her transferred to a couple of other schools. No error
(A: adjust herself well to; B: in fact; C: has had; D: transferred to; E: No error)

4. Catherine became so fed up with editing spelling and grammar mistakes of the books in a publishing company that she tried to change her career, but simultaneously worried of her single mother, whom she had to support. No error
(A: became so fed up with; B: spelling and grammar mistakes; C: that she tried to; D: worried of; E: No error)

5. The hard truth is that blockbuster movies, which usually show huge scale action and exploding scenes, is all about advertisement. No error
(A: truth is that; B: movies, which; C: show; D: is; E: No error)

6. The agency barely managed to understand what Sanders wanted before the contract; he preferred receiving cash up front to increase the annual bonus. No error
(A: barely; B: to understand; C: receiving; D: increase; E: No error)

7. When Sue went out to pick up the paper, there was a girl or a young boy wanted to talk to her. No error
(A: pick up; B: girl or; C: wanted; D: talk to; E: No error)

8. Individuals who work in professions that have enormous interactions with other people have a tendency of receiving high stress and so remain quiet after work. No error
(A: who work in; B: that have; C: of receiving; D: after work; E: No error)

9. The mountain is covered with snow and full of climbers all year round; family climbers
(A: is covered with; B: full of; C: all year round; family climbers)

enjoy nature fill with trees (D) on the mid ridges, and trained climbers enjoy the steep cliffs approaching the highest peak. No error (E)

10. Those who indulge in (A) the role playing computer games can show paranoia and lack the passion for (B) work and study because the virtual world can compensate for (C) what you (D) cannot achieve in reality. No error (E)

11. The circling pattern of a group ritual (A) is associated with (B) protection from and preparation of (C) invasion, since each participant can carefully watch the vicinity of his circling angle (D). No error (E)

12. During the dynasty (A), metal was made into (B) vessels, which were (C) soon made by wet clay (D). No error (E)

13. When Curt was introduced to (A) Jeff's fiancé, he could not help feel (B) jealous of (C) Jeff by the young look (D) of the fiancé. No error (E)

14. That students who (A) are exposed to the smells (B) from snacks in the classroom will not be able to concentrate with (C) the lesson is why Tim does not agree on (D) school's plan. No error (E)

15. Since the economic situation (A) was not satisfactorily (B), the new chief of the police department dispensed with (C) the formal (D) welcoming ceremony. No error (E)

16. Even though (A) Mel graduated from one of top ten universities, he is very susceptible for (B) rumors and makes a very poor investment decision on (C) the romantic ideas which he has only a glimpse of (D). No error (E)

17. The scientists know that it (A) is necessary to create (B) a matching equation (C) to make machine to work (D) accurately. No error (E)

18. Ted somehow feels that eating sweets (A) while working is conducive to increasing (B) his work performance and thus, has never been (C) in good shape (D). No error (E)

19. Even though (A) the Chinese government takes a census (B) regularly, it is hard to keep up with (C) increasing rate, rapidly occurring (D) during the census. No error (E)

20. The thought that she had to deal with the angry clients robbed her from sleep during the entire night. No error
(A: thought; B: with the angry clients; C: from sleep; D: entire; E: No error)

21. It is uncertain if the judges had already decided to favor the player of the host country, but certain that the silver medalist performed much better than did the gold medalist. No error
(A: if; B: had already decided; C: that; D: than did; E: No error)

22. The reason Timmy does not want to take one to one lessons is that he feels unnecessary to spend money on the lessons he has no problem understanding them. No error
(A: take; B: that; C: on; D: understanding them; E: No error)

23. Attempt of ignoring cultural differences does not save time in learning a language; it lengthens the time, since there are many expressions based on culture. No error
(A: of ignoring; B: learning; C: it; D: based on culture; E: No error)

24. Countries with high developed space technology have been preparing ways to protect the Earth from asteroids, which can be great threats to Earth. No error
(A: with high developed; B: have been preparing; C: asteroids, which; D: threats to; E: No error)

25. David took pride in his work, but his co-workers and supervisors were not satisfied about it and could not tell him the truth, because of his defensive nature. No error
(A: took pride in; B: but; C: satisfied about; D: defensive nature; E: No error)

26. Nina hated Jason not so much for his deceptive nature as for his surprisingly skilled business ability. No error
(A: hated; B: deceptive; C: as; D: surprisingly; E: No error)

27. As a manager, day and night time workers are notified by Tommy of their shifts and job details. No error
(A: a; B: day and night time workers are notified by Tommy; C: of; D: shifts and job details; E: No error)

28. Chris hated the feeling of rushing to all the museums, and shops in the beach area and coming back to the hotel inland on the same day. No error
(A: feeling of; B: museums, and shops; C: area and; D: on the same day; E: No error)

29. In the first couple of days, Naomi and Kim could not resist to shop, because all the products on the streets seemed cheap and real, but after buying to their hearts' content, they realized they had paid more than they would in the duty-free shops. No error
(A: resist to shop; B: cheap and real; C: to their hearts' content; D: had paid; E: No error)

30. Invited to the party was young workers from John's company, old ladies from Sally's supermarket, and a party band in alien looking costumes. No error
(A: was; B: supermarket, and; C: in; D: looking; E: No error)

REAL TEST 6

1. The trip to the island was a serendipitous, and bonding experience for my family for the
A B C
tiring summer time. No error
D E

2. With Victor's help, Jane finished eating in bed, so she felt like to owe Victor a favor. No error
A B C D E

3. Kathrine is alleged to care for her children to the extreme level; she calls the school if
A B C
they do not reply her message immediately.No error
D E

4. Many English words are derived from other languages, such as Chinese and French, but,
A
ironically, many non-native English speakers relearn the English pronunciations of the
B C
words again. No error
D E

5. Vincent had a very shy and quiet quality to that many were reversely attracted . No error
A B C D E

6. Find the right road was not easy although they had bought a very detailed map before the
A B C
trip, which described each and every road in the city. No error
D E

7. For the trip to Europe with Amy, Tess, and Jim and his sister after the final term, Suzanne
A
prepared a schedule table so that they could make sure to not miss any important
B C
attraction. No error
D E

8. Word and grammar books are the first one to study when students start to prepare for any
A B C D
official test. No error
E

9. Jeff suggested to play basketball together, but I did not want to go outside in such a late
A B C
hour, so I told him that I already had an appointment. No error
D E

10. Having quit the job, Jason established his own shop that was intolerable for the owners
A B C
of his previous shop because the two shops were very close and sold almost the same
D

products. No error
E

11. The sales manager Lucy had all the salesmen wear suits that they liked, and go directly to
A B C
the promotion site, not to the company. No error
D E

12. After many big disasters caused by corruption and loose monitoring system, most citizens
A B
in the country have become oblivious about the insecure surroundings. No error
C D E

13. The movie director, Steven Spielberg, made the famous alien movie, ET, which brought him
A B
international fame, but other alien movies after it did not have as much impact. No error
C D E

14. The fast, long movement of tubes is the best feature of the water park, even though most
A B
people feel it is too expensive to ride and watch others enjoy it. No error
C D E

15. Shawn will take the place of the two managers of the old companies when the merger
A B C
takes place. No error
D E

16. Indicating the mistakes she made in her writing, her husband was convinced by her how
A B
necessary it was for her to be completely alone in a remote place when she was working.
C D
No error
E

17. Children in Philippines do not have the same situation as those in other countries nearby;
A B
they are suffering not only from poverty, also from natural disasters such as typhoon,
C
which takes away food, houses, and loved ones. No error
D E

18. Of 200 snake species native from Japan, only 2 percent of them are fatal to humans. No error
A B C D E

19. Lindsay does not like teachers who interfere with reading practice by explaining the
A
definition of words; she believes that it is more important to catch the meaning of the
B
whole passage, and therefore there should be no interruption in the way. No error
C D E

20. Even though some of my friends have dogs excreting on the streets, they don't pick up
A B
what is left by dogs and left the scene. No error
C D E

21. On one summer morning, Jessica was going to work earlier than usual, having a cool
A
breeze blown in her face and listening to pop music when she saw Jack in front of a bull
B C

statue in the blue shirt. No error
D E

22. A series of books called *The Lord of the Rings* were made into movies, but many said
A B
movies were not much interesting than the books. No error
C D E

23. Many stories of Greek myth have been accepted by some of contemporary historians
A B
because scientists and historians cannot attest to the stance that the stories never happen.
C D
No error
E

24. Most of language instructors in ESL program agree with that students need to succeed
A
in applying simple and easy sentences, since English works in harmony, not in each and
B C
individual sentence. No error
D E

25. The defense department decided not to install the stealth function on the fighters because
A B
it found out that the radar systems could still have reacted to the fighters even with the
C D
function. No error
E

26. Even though Sammy had lived in China for eight years, he was far from adapting himself
A B
to the real Chinese culture when his sister visited him, because he had hard learned the
C D
Chinese language or met the local people. No error
E

27. Full House, the title of the TV talk show, may conjure up the poker game, but the show is
A B C
about the relationships among the family members of various celebrities. No error
D E

28. Listening to Clare talking about her old classmate, who got successful and made a large
A
amount of money, Ron felt jealous and spent the whole night figuring out the way to cope
B C D
with the jealousy. No error
E

29. Watching David play the harmonica, Jen was surprised, "How could a guy over 70 years
A B C
old have such healthy functioning lungs?" No error
D E

30. The ex-president Bill Clinton was scheduled to visit my school and gave a speech in the
A B C D
McFerrin Hall. No error
E

REAL TEST 7

1. With a minor infection in the eyes, Kirill enjoyed the party to his hearts content, but the
   A B C
   next morning when he woke up, he found out that the infection had gotten worse. No error
   D E
2. Although the Japanese government and many organizations regarding human rights
   A B
   pled, the Singapore government detained the two Japanese who were suspected of drug
   C D
   traffickers. No error
   E
3. Zooming in the camera, Dr. Hugh by no means had an intention to look at the group of
   A B C
   ladies, but was testing its functions. No error
   D E
4. When Linda walked out of the airport security area, she took notice of many
   A B C
   photographers and reporters, waiting to ask her about the scandal. No error
   D E
5. That rice is to Japanese as wheat is to American does not apply for Chinese because the
   A B C
   preferred food differs between region to region. No error
   D E
6. His day job was a means of sustaining his family, but the short stories he wrote after
   A B
   work was a way to realize his dream. No error
   C D E
7. Ellen strongly protested against the school's policy to keep the students at school after
   A B
   classes and have them finished homework if they did not do it. No error
   C D E
8. Most people work most of days to make a living, but they don't know they can be
   A
   successful if they find a goal and focus on it even though they don't earn anything in the
   B C
   beginning. No error
   D E
9. Mikhail, for fear of getting blamed and fired, called his supervisor first, thus explained
   A B
   why the customers put negative remarks on Yelp website. No error
   C D E

10. Despite of [A] the great offer, Singh had to reconsider about becoming [B] an associate because [C] the company seemed fraught with [D] many obstacles to prevent efficient communication. No error [E]

11. When Jiang decided to resume her study abroad just a couple of months shy to [A] her 40's birthday and posted [B] the news online, many friends of hers, who were house wives, did [C] not respond; they could not understand why she chose to study [D] when she was supposed to meet a man and get married. No error [E]

12. Neither the car nor [A] the bike belong to [B] Henry; he uses public transportations and does not [C] have to worry about [D] alcohol intake during the party. No error [E]

13. Devoid [A] a true successor of [B] Hui descent, the members of Hui reserve project were getting worn out [C] when the chairman decided to tell [D] the congressman that the project would be delayed. No error [E]

14. The marshal intervened with [A] the gang related [B] conflict in the area with [C] the offer of [D] a peaceful negotiation. No error [E]

15. The access code to [A] the wireless network [B] of the school is [C] well known to [D] the students. No error [E]

16. Managers blamed workers; workers, poor display; board members, mismanagement [A] for the decline of customers, but the CEO June [B] thought that all of these factors had been [C] working of [D] tandem. No error [E]

17. Ms. Jenna is seemed [A] to have all chemistry knowledge at her fingertips [B]; she doesn't even hesitate and supports [C] firmly for her stance [D] when she is challenged by students with fairly advanced questions. No error [E]

18. While [A] Jack and Wendy were discussing about [B] their wedding plan, he was caught off guard [C] and frustrated by [D] her question about the plan for a new car. No error [E]

19. The disastrous accident of the ship Titanic [A] had a significant impact not only on [B] ship building and [C] safety regulations, also [D] movie and book productions. No error [E]

20. Rene's cat Oscar is not tractable and has Rene devote her full attention of taking care of
A B
him; otherwise he excretes everywhere in the house. No error
C D E

21. Although Chen tried to be fair for her team members, she couldn't afford to the tickets to
A B C D
the conference for everyone in the Bahamas. No error
E

22. Putting the frosting between the nose and the mouth of the face shaped cake destroyed by
A B
handling too carelessly were Lucy, the baker and mother of the one year old boy, whom
C D
she made the cake for. No error
E

23. Matt has a tendency to exaggerate what he hears and if he has to, he would change the
A B C
protagonist of the story as if he experienced everything. No error
D E

24. Billy, my cousin's dog, is attuned to the life in the wild; it sleeps well under a tree and
A B
very sensitive to the slight movement in the surroundings. No error
C D E

25. The reason the criminal dedicated so much to taking care of poor people was because he
A B C
could find a possible target. No error
D E

26. Many students find it surprising that so many words are synonymous with the words in
A B C
the question parts that they need to figure the sentence structure. No error
D E

27. To Murdock's huge success in online game business, his friends, as well as many other
A
close and distant family members, were at a loss and did not make a contact to him at first,
B C
even though they all wanted to be the first to congratulate him on the news. No error
D E

28. Even though blind, sensors in his ears and the cap are used by Sean to keep pace with or
A B C
be better than other swimmers. No error
D E

29. The movie director Steven Spielberg's movie Catch Me if You Can is based on the life
A B
story of a real person, who started forging checks when he was a minor. No error
C D E

30. Moving to a small apartment, Henry has been struggling to make room for the treehouse
A B C
for his cat, which does not sleep and cries during the night without it. No error
D E

REAL TEST 1 ANSWERS

1. D 把 for 改成 on

   Idiom in use wreak havoc on（给……造成混乱）

2. E

   Idiom in use succeed to（继承，继任）

3. C 把 generously 改成 generous

   这里由于修饰主语 he，因此必须使用形容词。

   Idiom in use differ from（与……不同）

4. C 把 would have walked 改成 had been walking

   此处应使用过去完成时以表达事情发生的前后顺序。

   Idiom in use cannot help but（不得不），at the sight of（看见……时）

5. B 把 about 改成 for

   由于来自加拿大的老师不止一个，所以 Chris 作为用以辨识的名字是关键信息，因此这里不能使用逗号。

   Idiom in use be responsible for（对……负责）

6. B 把 committed 改成 would commit

   此处时态应为过去将来时，因此做如上修改。

   Idiom in use commit to ...ing（致力于……）

7. B 把 was 改成 were

   就近原则。

   Idiom in use neither A nor B（既不是 A，也不是 B），be responsible for（对……负责）

8. C 去掉 and

   and 和 making 同时使用是错误的，相当于句子中同时使用了两个连词。

9. A 把 with 改成 to

   Idiom in use be equivalent to（等同于）

10. D 把 emptied 改成 empty

left 后应接一个形容词，这里可以使用 empty。one of 后应接名词复数，而 one 为该词组的核心名词，所以 A 是正确的，B 的用法正确。

Idiom in use a stretch of（一片）

11. B 把 like 改成 likely

Idiom in use be likely to（可能）

12. B 在 result 后插入 in

Idiom in use result in (引起，导致)，have an effect on (对……有影响)

13. E

Idiom in use be aware of（意识到），put forth（提出）

14. A 把 with 改成 to

Idiom in use contrary to（和……相反），delve into（钻研）

15. B 把 dense 改成 densely

这里 dense 修饰的 packed 为动词，因此应该使用副词。

Idiom in use refrain from ...ing (制止，克制)

16. D 把 due to 改成 for

Idiom in use be known for（因……而众所周知）

17. E

the number of 做主语的时候动词应使用第三人称单数，因此选项 C 正确，选项 B 的主语是 students，因此也是正确的。

18. E

hate 后可以接动词不定式、名词或动名词，而 escape 后接名词或动名词。

19. C 把 insists 改成 insist

当用 a number of 修饰名词并做主语的时候，主语核心词是该词组修饰的名词，因此谓语动词应使用复数。

20. D 把 us 改成 them

主语是 people，因此不能使用 us。

Idiom in use be obsessed with（对…… 着迷）

21. B 去掉 buy

不能把 buy 改成 buying，最好的方法是 to+ 动词或者 for+ 名词。

22. E

在选项 A 中 rapidly 修饰 grinding，而 grind in 为固定词组，此处正确。在选项 B 中由于表达的都是 food，应用物主代词，故此处正确。选项 C burst 的过去式所写是 burst，故正确并且选项 C 和 D 连在一起的 burst into tears 是正确的表达 。

23. A 把 their 改成 its

主语为 bullfrog，此处物主代词使用错误。

Idiom in use prey on（捕食），be supposed to（应该）

24. D 把 of slipping 改成 to slip

Idiom in use have a tendency to (有倾向)，be covered with (盖着，覆着)

25. D 把 from 改成 of

Idiom in use instead of (代替，而不是)

26. B 把 has said 改成 said

时态使用错误，A 选项中的“A couple of months ago ”提示本句时态应为过去式。

Idiom in use be done with（受够了）

27. D 把 feels 改成 has felt

since + 时间这种模式用以引导完成时态，所以句子需要使用现在完成时。

Idiom in use a pang of（一阵）

28. C 把 he told 改成 did he tell

not until 前置为倒装结构，因此主句应使用倒装，这里为部分倒装，因此将助动词 did 提前与 not until 共同构成倒装结构。

Idiom in use in regard to (关于……)

29. A 把 about 改成 to

Idiom in use refer to (指的是……)

30. C 去掉 to

make 后接动词原形。

Idiom in use a critic of（关于……的评论家），be interested in（对……感兴趣）

REAL TEST 2 ANSWERS

1. B 把 to participate 改成 participating

reject 为及物动词，后接名词或动名词；C 选项正确，insist 后接虚拟语气，另外此处的 should 可以省略。

Idiom in use participate in（参加）

2. A 把 stang 改成 stung

Idiom in use be responsible for（对……负有责任），in case of（万一）

3. C 把 being 改成 since the smart phones are

此处考查逻辑主语结构，being helpful 从句子结构来看，其逻辑主语为 most parents，但是根据句子的意思来看，其主语应该是 smart phones，因此 C 选项处应加一个主语以使句子更加清晰，避免歧义。

Idiom in use be helpful for（对……有利），be harmful to（对……有害）

4. D 把 search 改成 search for

句子的意思是动物找食物。

Idiom in use search for（寻找）

5. C 把 need 改成 needs

which 在句中指代 technology，因此应使用 needs；选项 C 中 which 用来指代前文的 technology，正确。

6. D 把 active 改成 actively

active 这里用来修饰 introducing 是错误的，应使用副词。

Idiom in use acclimate to ...ing (适应)

7. D 把 our 改成 the person's

句中分号前后的人称应保持一致以表示并列。

8. B 把 of 改成 with

Idiom in use be concerned with (关心)，be interested in (对……感兴趣)

9. A 把 which flooded 改成 flooding

当 which 用在一个完整的句子之后的时候，它所指代的是一个名词还是前面的整个句子不是很清楚。如果做如上修改的话，可以非常清晰地表达句子的本意。

Idiom in use suffer through (遭受，挨过去)

10. A 去掉逗号

“her brother”是关键信息，用来修饰 “Sam”，因此这里不能使用逗号。 如果将句子改成 ...Sam，her brother，if he was willing to... 那么“her brother”是辅助信息，这样就必须使用逗号了。

Idiom in use be willing to (愿意)，partake in (参加)

11. B 去掉 to

oppose 可做及物动词，不需要使用介词 to。

12. D 在 Canadian 前加入 that of

比较的双方不对等，因此做如上修改以清晰表达原句的意图。

Idiom in use liken A to B 把 A 比作 B

13. A 把 with 改成 for

Idiom in use be available for (可供……之用)

14. C 把 to ruin 改成 ruining

resist 为及物动词，后接名词或动名词。

15. E

Idiom in use in one's way (挡了……的路)

16. B 在 put on 前插入 was

B 处应使用被动语态，因此做如上修改。

Idiom in use put on hold （搁置，延迟)

17. A 把 is 改成 was

句子结构为 it is not until...that，整句的时态为过去式，因此做如上修改。

18. A 把 of 改成 about

Idiom in use be worried about (担心)，on time (准时)

19. E

选项 A 为固定词组；选项 B 都是不可数名词；选项 C 中副词修饰动词 become；

选项 D 中工作的名称用在动词后的时候可以不使用冠词；因此选项 E 为正确答案。

Idiom in use by virtue of (由于，凭借……的力量)

20. A 把 has 改成 had

时态使用错误，这里应使用过去完成时以表达事情发生的先后顺序。

Idiom in use a series of (一系列)，come into existence (成立，建立)

21. B 把 in 改成 with

Idiom in use preoccupy with (全神贯注于……)

22. B 把 as 改成 to be

Chris 表达的是他的态度而不是他的工作，所以这里应使用 to be 而不是 as。

Idiom in use be indifferent to (对……不以为意)

23. C 把 better than 改成 to

如果在比较结构中使用了 superior，那么就不能再使用 than 而应该改用 to，以构成词组 superior to； not only 需要与 but 或者分号共同使用，所以选项 B 正确；比较双方是 army 和 armies，所以选项 D 中使用 those of 是正确的。

24. C 在 competition 后使用 than

用 than 替代句中的逗号。

25. D 把 in 改成 at

Idiom in use ill at ease (局促不安)

26. B 把 easiness 改成 ease

Idiom in use put someone at ease (使……不拘束)

27. A 去掉 of

despite 是介词，可以直接接名词。

28. A 把 in 改成 on

Idiom in use insist on (坚持)

29. A 把 as 改成 to be

句子表达的是 John 的处境而不是工作，所以这里不能使用 as。

Idiom in use preoccupy with (全神贯注于……)，participate in (参加)

30. C 把 with 改成 in

Idiom in use in favor of (赞成)，engage in (参与)

REAL TEST 3 ANSWERS

1. C 把 hand 改成 hands

   Idiom in use hands-on （亲身实践）

2. B 把 from 改成 of

   Idiom in use rid A of B（把 B 从 A 去掉）

3. D 把 of 改成 about

   Idiom in use be accessible to（可接近的，可用的），be concerned about（关心）

4. C 把 leave 改成 leaving

   be used to 意为习惯……，此处意思与句意相符，但是该词组后应使用名词或动名词，因此做如上修改。

   Idiom in use object to（反对）

5. A 在 consists 后插入 of

   Idiom in use consist of（由……组成）

6. A 把 is 改成 are

   主语为 workers，动词应使用复数。

   Idiom in use be involved in（涉及，卷入）。

7. C 在 dilemma 和 instead 之间插入分号

   instead 不是连词，因此不能用于连接句子。

   Idiom in use take into account（考虑），deal with（应对，处理）

8. A 把 for 改成 to

   Idiom in use be acceptable to（对……可以接受），deal with（应对，处理）

9. C 在 bought 前使用 had

   时态使用错误，此处应使用过去完成时以表达时间发生的顺序。

   Idiom in use knock over（撞翻），by mistake（错误地），insulate against（防止）

10. E

comprise 为及物动词，不需要使用介词。

11. C 把 a friend with 改成 friends with

Idiom in use make friends with (与……交朋友)

12. A 把 to persuade 改成 of persuading

Idiom in use be capable of (能够)，be able to (能够)

13. D 去掉 for

pay 的直接宾语是 fee 而 for 后接的名词则是 pay fee 的目的。

Idiom in use suggest...ing (建议)

14. D 把 girl 改成 girl's' 或 that of any normal girl

比较结构，需做如上修改以使比较双方具有可比性。

Idiom in use be negligent of (疏忽)，put away (收起来，放好，储存)

15. D 把 calling 改成 to call

Idiom in use be capable of (能够)，pay for (为……付钱)，have no choice but to (只能)

16. B 把 because of 改成 to

Idiom in use attribute to (归因于)，contribute to (有助于，促成)

17. C 把 at 改成 into

这里不能使用介词 at 而应该使用 into 表达检查的意思。

Idiom in use to one's surprise (让……惊讶的是)，take care of (照顾)，look into (检查，检验)

18. A 在 contact with 前加入 in

Idiom in use be in contact with (与……保持联络)，feed on (以……为食)

19. D 在 those who 前加入 that of

此为比较结构，做如上修改以使得比较双方具有可比性。

Idiom in use be prone to (易于)，relate to (与……相关)

20. A 把 to 改成 up

Idiom in use be fond of (喜欢)，look up (查找)，be sure of (确信)

21. D 代词指代不明确

he 可以指代前面两人中的任何一个，因此需要明确的使用名字以避免歧义。

22. C 把 to visit 改成 visiting

Idiom in use postpone...ing (推迟)

23. E

Idiom in use give way to (让路)

24. C 把 them 改成 it

指示代词使用错误，因此做如上修改。

Idiom in use be made of (用……造成)

25. C 把 handedly 改成 handed

Idiom in use be caught red-handed (被当场抓住)，give a break (休息一下)

26. A 把 about 改成 off

Idiom in use see off (出发)，come across (遇到)

27. E

Idiom in use A as well as B (也)

28. B 把 to 改成 with

Idiom in use be familiar with (熟悉)，be familiar to (被某人熟悉)

29. B 把 could have entered 改成 could enter

根据句子的意思，此处不能使用虚拟语气，因此做如上修改。

Idiom in use thanks to (幸亏)，in time (及时)

30. B 在 Korean 前加入 so

just as，so（too）为固定搭配。

Idiom in use just as...，so (就像……一样，也)

REAL TEST 4 ANSWERS

1. D 把 indefinite 改成 indecisive

   选词错误

   Idiom in use be satisfied with （满意）

2. D 把 crossed 改成 cross

   此处为并列结构，因此应使用动词不定式。

   Idiom in use be at large (在逃，逍遥法外)

3. D 在 succeed 后加入 to

   Idiom in use make an excuse (找借口)，succeed to (继承)

4. B 在 characters 和 and 之间插入逗号

   在列举三个或多于三个事物的时候，需使用结构 A，B，and C，而两个的时候则不需要。

   Idiom in use be worth...ing (值得)

5. A 把 for 改成 of

   Idiom in use be certain of (确信)，hand in (上交，递交)

6. E

   Idiom in use hand out (分发)

7. B 把 suspiciously 改成 suspicious

   look 后应使用形容词。

8. B 把 studying 改成 to study

   Idiom in use decide to (决定)，be similar to (与……相似)

9. C 把 how the house should be big 改成 how big the house should be

10. C 把 fastly 改成 fast

    fast 本身既是形容词又是副词。

    Idiom in use by order of (奉……命令)，under control （处于控制之下）

11. A 把 to 改成 of

Idiom in use be oblivious of（忘却），keep up with（跟上）

12. B 把 he or she has 改成 they have

因为主语 expatriates 是复数，因此做如上修改。

Idiom in use in pursuit of（追求）

13. C 把 out 改成 off

call out 意为“大声喊或命令”，而根据句子原意，此处应为“取消”，因此做如上修改。

Idiom in use supplant A with B（用 B 取代 A)，call off（取消），put off（推迟，拖延）

14. D 把 their 改成 its

这里的 their 指的是 young generation，因此应使用单数。

Idiom in use dispossess A of B（使 A 不再拥有 B）

15. D 把 in 改成 to

主语为 effects，所以 B 正确。

Idiom in use in need of（需要），pay attention to...ing（注意）

16. C 把 to ascribe 改成 ascribed

这里使用词组 ascribe to 的被动式，用以表达句中的意思由于 jet lag 导致的 bad conditions。

Idiom in use ascribe to（把……归于……)

17. E

Idiom in use depend on（依靠）

18. C 把 it 改成 doing so

这里不能用 it 来指代 joining the website 而应该使用 doing so。

Idiom in use qualify for（合格）

19. C 把 to talk 改成 talking

选项 D 中，原句应为 someone who is accused of，而 who/that/which + am/are/is 可以省略，因此此处正确。

Idiom in use have a hard time...ing（在……方面有困难），be accused of（被起诉，被批评）

20. A 把 of 改成 in

Idiom in use be engaged in (从事于)

21. C 把 it 改成 the movie

能够打动 Sam 的既有可能是 the movie 也有可能是 the situation of talking，句中的表达不清晰，因此做如上修改。

Idiom in use ward off (避免)，in vain (徒劳)

22. B 把 suffering 改成 suffering from

Idiom in use enter into (开始)，suffer from (受……折磨)，on the basis of (基于)

23. E

根据句子的意思，选项 A 正确；need 后可以接动词不定式，因为 need 既可以做情态动词也可以做普通动词，因此选项 B 正确；选项 C 中 的词组 have something done 为正确用法；选项 D 中 keep doing 也是正确用法。

24. B 把 to have 改成 having

Idiom in use in addition to (除……之外还)，consider...ing (考虑)

25. E

选项 A 中，method 后可以使用介词 of 或者 to；选项 D 中，使用过去完成时符合句中的时态关系。

26. D 把 about 改成 for

Idiom in use account for (解释)，deal with (应对)

27. E

选项 A 考查逻辑主语结构，replaced 的逻辑主语与句中的主语 Jonathan 一致。

Idiom in use abide by (遵守)

28. B 把 have 改成 has

句中主语 strategy 为第三人称单数，因此做如上修改。

Idiom in use focus on (致力于……)

29. C 把 at 改成 to

这里 look at 的意思与句子的意图不符，因此做如上修改。

Idiom in use look forward to...ing (期待)，look to (朝……看去)

30. D 在 regardless 后加 of

Idiom in use be in charge of (负责)，in front of (在……前)，regardless of (不考虑)

REAL TEST 5 ANSWERS

1. D 把 in 改成 for

   Idiom in use instill in (灌注)，take responsibility for (承担责任)

2. D 把 returning 改成 to return

   Idiom in use excel in (在……方面胜过)，decide to (决定)，return something to (归还)

3. D 把 transferred 改成 transfer

   have someone do 是固定搭配。

   Idiom in use adjust to (调整)，transfer to (转去)

4. D 把 of 改成 about

   Idiom in use be fed up with (厌烦)，worry about (担心)

5. D 把 is 改成 are

   主语 movies 为复数，因此动词做如上修改。

6. D 把 increase 改成 increasing

   句中对比的双方应是 receiving 和 increasing，因此做如上修改。

   Idiom in use prefer A to B (喜欢 A 多于 B)

7. C 把 wanted 改成 who wanted

   第二句以 there is 开头，因此动词需要使用 who 做主语。

8. C 把 of receiving 改成 to receive

   Idiom in use work in profession (从事某项职业)，have a tendency to (倾向于)

9. D 把 fill 改成 filled

   Idiom in use be covered with (盖着，覆着)，be full of (充满)，be filled with (充满)

10. D 把 you 改或 they

主语是 those who，因此当在句中重复的时候，应选择代词 they。

Idiom in use indulge in（沉溺于），passion for（对……的激情），compensate for（补偿）

11. C 把 of 改成 for

Idiom in use be associated with（与……关联），prepare for（为……做准备）

12. D 把 by 改成 of

Idiom in use be made into（被制成），be made of（由……制成）

13. B 把 feel 改成 feeling

Idiom in use: cannot help...ing（禁不住），be jealous of（嫉妒）

14. C 把 with 改成 on

本句为 that 引导的名词性从句，主句动词为 is，所以选项 A 正确；有时候 on 用来连接问题相关的计划，比如日常和问题，所以选项 D 也是正确的。

Idiom in use be exposed to（暴露），be able to（能够），concentrate on（集中注意力）

15. B 把 satisfactorily 改成 satisfactory

这里应使用形容词。

Idiom in use dispense with（摒弃）

16. B 把 for 改成 to

Idiom in use be susceptible to（对……敏感），make a decision（做决定）

17. D 去掉 to

make machine work 是正确的结构。

18. E

Idiom in use be conducive to...ing（有助于），be in good shape（处于良好状态）

19. D 把 rapidly occurring 改成 which rapidly occurs

从句子结构来看 rapidly occurring 的主语应该是 it，但是这不符合句子的意图，rapidly occurring 的真正逻辑主语应该是 rate，因此在这里做如上的修改。

Idiom in use keep up with（跟上）

20. C 把 from 改成 of

Idiom in use deal with（应对），rob A of B（从 A 手中夺走 B）

21. A 把 if 改成 whether

if 引导名词从句不能作为句子主语或者补语，uncertain 已经表达了不确定性，所以 if 是多余的。

22. D 去掉 them

这里的 them 指代前文的 lessons，此处可以省略。

Idiom in use spend time/money on (花时间 / 钱做某事)

23. A 把 of ignoring 改成 to ignore

Idiom in use attempt to (尝试)，be based on (基于)

24. A 把 high 改成 highly

由于修饰 developed，因此这里应使用副词而不是形容词。

Idiom in use a threat to (威胁)

25. C 把 about 改成 with

Idiom in use take pride in (以……为傲)，be satisfied with (满意)

26. E

Idiom in use not so much A as B (与其说 A 不如说 B)

27. B 把 day and night time workers are notified by Tommy 改成 Tommy notifies day and night workers

第二句应以 Tommy 做主语开头。

28. B 去掉逗号

当列举两个事物的时候，不需要使用逗号。

29. A 把 to shop 改成 shopping

Idiom in use resist...ing (抵制)，to one's heart content (心满意足)

30. A 把 was 改成 were

倒装句的主语是 workers，ladies，and a band，因此动词应使用复数。

REAL TEST 6 ANSWERS

1. B 去掉逗号或者 and

当列举两个事物使用 and 进行连接的时候，不需要使用逗号；而当这两个事物具有同样功能的时候，只能使用逗号进行连接。

2. C 把 to owe 改成 owing

Idiom in use finish...ing (完成)，feel like...ing (想要)

3. D 在 reply 后加入 to

在选项 C 中，分号可以起到连词的作用，连接两个句子。

Idiom in use care for (喜欢，关心)，reply to (回复，回答)

4. D 去掉 again

句中已经有 relearn，有重复的意思，因此不再需要使用 again

Idiom in use derive from (由……起源)

5. B 把 that 改成 which

使用 that 引导从句的时候，介词不能前置，因此做如上修改。

6. A 把 find 改成 finding

选项 A 中 find 为动词，不能用做主语，因此改为动名词；选项 B 为连词，此处用来连接两个句子，用法正确；选项 C 中使用过去完成时，清晰地表达了事情发展的时间顺序；which 可以指代副词短语前的名词，而 before the trip 是一个副词短语，因此选项 D 正确。

7. C 把 to not miss 改成 not to miss

not 的正确位置应在 to miss 之前。

选项 A 中，因为有三个事物，因此使用逗号正确；Jim and his sister 可以作为一个事物来理解，因此 A 正确。

Idiom in use make sure (核实，保证)

8. C 把 one 改成 ones

主语 word and grammar books 是复数，所以 C 处应使用 ones 进行指代。

Idiom in use prepare for (做准备)

9. A 把 to play 改成 playing

Idiom in use suggest...ing / suggest to someone to (建议)

10. C 把 for 改成 to

选项 A 中，由于 quit 这个动作发生在 established 之前，因此应使用现在分词的完成时。

Idiom in use be intolerable to (对……是无法忍受的)

11. C 去掉逗号

当两句话共用同一个主语并用 and 进行连接的时候，无须使用逗号；选项 D 中的两部分在句中功能是相同的，它们之间不需要使用 and 进行连接，可以直接采用文中的模式用逗号连接

Idiom in use have someone do (让某人做……)

12. D 把 about 改成 to

Idiom in use be oblivious to (注意不到)

13. A 去掉逗号

当职务在名字之前使用的时候，不需要使用逗号。

14. D 把 it 改成 them

选项 A 正确，功能相同的两部分并列时，可以使用 and 或逗号连接；主语 movement 为单数，因此选项 B 正确；选项 C 中 it 指代 to ride，因此正确；选项 D 中的 it 实际上指代的是前文的 tubes，此处为指示代词的选择错误。

15. E

Idiom in use take place (发生)

16. B 把 her husband was convinced by her 改成 she convinced her husband

逻辑主语错误，indicating 的主语应该是 she，而不是 her husband，因此做如上修改。

17. C 在 also 前加入 but

also 不是连词，因此不能用来连接句子。

选项 B 中用分号连接句子的用法是正确的；选项 D 中，当列举三个或三个以上事物的时候，应该在每个事物之后使用逗号。

Idiom in use suffer from (遭受)，the same... as (与……同样的)

18. B 把 from 改成 to

Idiom in use native to (原产于……)

19. D 把 in 改成 on

interruption 和 in the way 同时使用造成了重复的表达。

选项 B 和 C 分别是两个句子相连接，文中使用了分号和 and，为正确的用法；选项 C 中使用副词 therefore 用来强调句意。

Idiom in use interfere with (干预)，in the way (造成不便)，on the way (在途中)

20. D 把 left 改成 leave

句中使用的时态是现在时，因此做如上修改。

21. D 把 in the blue shirt 移到 Jack 后

Idiom in use have something done (让人做某事)

22. C 把 much 改成 more

本句为对比，因此应使用 more 构成比较级。

Idiom in use a series of (一系列)

23. D 把 happen 改成 happened

事件发生在过去，因此应该使用一般过去时。

Idiom in use attest to (证实，证明)

24. A 去掉 with

词组 agree with 后接名词，而 agree that 则可以直接引导从句，因此去掉 with。在选项 D 中，in harmony (adverb)，not in sentence (adverb) 这两个部分在句中的功能相同，只需要用逗号进行连接。

Idiom in use agree with (同意)，succeed in (在……中获得成功)

25. D 去掉 have 并改成 react to。

此处不能使用虚拟语气。

选项 C 中 it 指代 department，属正确用法。

Idiom in use react to (对……做出反应)

26. D 把 hard 改成 hardly

Idiom in use far from (远非……)，adapt to (使适应……)

27. E

在选项 A 中需要使用逗号，因为句中的两个名词不符合可以省略逗号的条件（职位 + 名字，或者作品 + 作品名称）

Idiom in use conjure up (凭空想象出……)

28. E

选项 B 正确，因为 jealous 是形容词。

Idiom in use listen + someone + do/doing (听 到 某 人 做 某 事)，spend time/money (on)...ing (花时间 / 钱做某事)，cope with (对付……).

29. D 把 healthy 改成 healthily

句中 healthy 用来修饰动词 functioning，此处应使用副词，因此做如上修改。

30. C 把 gave 改成 give

句子时态为一般过去式。在选项 A 中，因为可以有很多前总统，因此 Bill Cliton 作为关键信息出现，因此此处不能使用逗号。

REAL TEST 7 ANSWERS

1. C 把 hearts 改成 heart's

Idiom in use to one's heart's content (令人心满意足)

2. D 在 of 后加入 being

此处应加入 being，用来表达这两个日本人是因为被怀疑“是”运毒者的意思。

Idiom in use be suspected of (被怀疑……)

3. C 把 to look 改成 of looking

Idiom in use have an intention of (想要)，by no means (决不)，zoom in (放大)

4. D 把 waiting 改成 who had been waiting

此处为逻辑主语问题，从结构上看原句的动词 waiting 的逻辑主语应该是 she，但是这样与原句的要表达意思不相符，因此加入 who had been 用来明确其主语是 photographers and reporters，以避免歧义。

5. D 把 between 改成 from

选项 A 正确，此为 that 引导的名词性从句；而选项 C 是 that 引导的名词性从句的动词。

Idiom in use A is to B as(what) C is to D (A 对于 B 相当于 C 对于 D)，differ from (与……不同)

6. C 把 was 改成 were

此处 be 动词的主语是 stories，因此应使用复数形式。

Idiom in use (a) means of (一种方式)

7. C 把 finished 改成 finish

Idiom in use have someone do (让某人做某事)

8. E

Idiom in use make a living (谋生)，focus on (致力于)

9. B 把 thus 改成 and

在选项 B 处，逗号前后分别为两个句子，因此需要用连词进行连接，而 thus 是个副词，因此做如上修改。

Idiom in use for fear of (为了避免……)

10. A 去掉 of

despite 后不需要介词

Idiom in use be fraught with (充满……)

11. A 把 to 改成 of

Idiom in use shy of (对……有顾虑)

12. B 把 belong 改成 belongs

当使用 (n)either A (n)or B 结构的时候，动词的数遵循就近原则。

Idiom in use neither A nor B (A 和 B 都不……)，belong to (属于)，worry about (担心)

13. A 在 devoid 后加入 of

Idiom in use devoid of (缺乏)，successor of (……的继承人)，be worn out (筋疲力尽，磨损)

14. A 把 with 改成 in

Idiom in use intervene in (干预)

15. E

Idiom in use access to (有权使用)，be known to (为……所熟知)

16. D 把 of 改成 in

选项 A 中的动词 blamed 实际是重复使用的动词，因此在几个并列的部分当中省略了重复的 blamed，原句应该是 Managers blamed workers; workers blamed poor display; board members blamed mismanagement. 所以分号的使用是正确的；在选项 B 中，CEO 为职务，因此与 June 之间不需要使用逗号；在选项 C 中使用过去完成时表达事情发生的先后顺序，此处为正确用法。

Idiom in use in tandem (一起，同时)

17. A 把 is seemed 改成 seems

is 和 seems 这两个动词在句中功能相同，因此去掉其中一个。

Idiom in use at one's fingertips (了如指掌)

18. B 去掉 about

discuss 是及物动词，因此不需要介词。

Idiom in use catch off guard (使措手不及)

19. D 在 also 前加入 but

Idiom in use not only A but also B (不仅 A，而且 B)，impact on (对……冲击)

20. B 把 of taking 改成 to taking

otherwise 不是连词，因此在 otherwise 前使分号来连接前后两个句子。

Idiom in use devote to...ing (致力于)

21. D 去掉 to

afford 是及物动词，此处不需要使用介词。

Idiom in use be fair for (对……公平)，can afford (买得起)

22. C 把 were 改成 was

句中在 "baker and mother" 前只有一个定冠词 the，因此 Lucy 既是 baker，也是男孩的妈妈。

Idiom in use between A and B (在 A 和 B 之间)

23. C 把 would 改成 will

原句为 if 引导的条件状语从句，因此在时态搭配方面，从句使用一般现在时，主句使用一般将来时。

Idiom in use have a tendency to (倾向于)

24. C 在 very sensitive to 前加入 is

and 作为并列连词连接前后两个句子，选项 C 处缺少动词，因此做如上修改。

Idiom in use be attuned to (习惯于)，be sensitive to (对……敏感)

25. C 把 because 改成 that

原句结构为 the reason is that，此处名词性从句不能用 because 引导，应使用 that 引导。

Idiom in use dedicate to...ing (致力于)，take care of (照顾)

26. D 在 figure 后加入 out

Idiom in use be synonymous with (等同于)

27. C 把 make a contact to 改成 make contact with

当使用 as well as 连接两个以上的并列成分时，应使用逗号，因此选项 A 正确。

Idiom in use make contact with (和……接触)，at a loss (不知所措)，congratulate someone on sth. (因某事祝贺某人)

28. B 把 sensors in his ears and the cap are used by Sean 改成 Sean uses sensors in his ears and the cap

blind 的逻辑主语应为 Sean，因此做如上修改。

Idiom in use keep pace with (与……保持一致)

29. E

Idiom in use be based on (基于……)

30. A 把 moving 改成 having moved

由于 moved 这个动作发生在 has been struggling 之前，因此选项 A 处应使用现在完成时的分词形式以表达动作发生的顺序，因此做如上修改。

Idiom in use make room for (给……让出地方)

ALPHABETICAL ORDER OF 307 IDIOMS AND EXPRESSIONS

A

abide by 遵守 , 信守
access to 有权使用……
acclimate (oneself) to + noun 使……适应……
account for（数量或者比例上）占，导致，解释
a critic of 一个……的评论家
adapt to 使适应于……，使适合……
adhere to 遵循，依附
adjust (oneself) to 调整……
adjust (oneself) to + noun 调整……以适应……
affection = have an effect on 影响……
agree on 双方或多方在某件事情上取得一致
A is to B as(what) C is to D A 对于 B，相当于 C 对于 D
(a) means of ……的方法
a number of = many 很多
the number of ……的数量
a pang of 一阵
appeal to 向……投诉；向……呼吁；对……有吸引力
argue against 不赞成……
argue with 与……争辩
as a result of 结果，因此
a series of 一系列，一连串
a stretch of 一片
as well as 也 , 又
at a loss 不知所措，困惑
at hand 在手边，在附近，即将来临或者发生
a threat to 对……的威胁
at large 在逃
at one’s fingertips 了如指掌
attempt to 尝试，企图
attest to 证实……
at the sight of 看见……时
attribute... to 把某事归因于……

B

be able to (have an ability to) 能……
be acceptable to 对……可以接受
be accused of = accuse A of B 因……被起诉，批评
be accessible to 可接近，可用
be accustomed to (be used to)... ing 习惯于……
be acquainted with 对……熟悉
be associated with 与……联系在一起
be attuned to 使习惯于，使适应
be available for 可获得的，可用的，可看见的
be aware of 意识到，知道
be based on 基于
be capable of (have a capacity of) 能……
be concerned about 关心，挂念
be concerned with 参与，干预
be conducive to 有助于……
be covered with 被……掩盖 , 盖着，覆着
be convinced of 确信，认识到，对……深信不疑
be devoid of 缺乏……
be distinct from 与……有区别
be done with 处理，再也不……了
be engaged in 从事于……
be equipped with 装备……
be equivalent to 相等或相当于……
be exposed to 暴露于……之下
be familiar with / to (familiarize A with B) 熟悉……
be famous for= be renowned for 因……而著名
be far away from 远离……
be far from (never) 远非……
be fed up with 饱受……，厌烦……
be filled with 充满着……，怀着……
be fond of 喜欢……
be fraught with 充满……
be full of 充满……
be harmful to 对……有害
be helpful for 对……有帮助
be ill at ease 局促不安，心神不宁
be indifferent to/about 对…… 不关心

be inferior to 次于……
be superior to 优于……
be junior to 比……年轻 / 次
be senior to 比……年长 / 次
be interested in 对……感兴趣
be involved in 涉及，卷入，参与
be jealous of 妒忌
be known as 号称……，被认为是……
be known to be 被称为
be known for 因……而众所周知
be known to 为……所熟知
be likely to (be unlikely to) 很可能（不可能）……
belong to 属于……
be made into 被制成……
be made from 由……所做成（多用于原材料不易看出的情况）
be made of 用……制成
be made up of 由……组成
be married to 与……结婚
be native to = home to 原产于
be negligent of (about) 在……上存在疏漏
be oblivious of 忘记了……
be oblivious to 没有注意到，没有察觉到
be obsessed with 痴迷于……
be opposed to(opposite to/ oppose) 反对……
be prone to 易于……的
be regarded as 被视为……
be regarded to be 被认为是……
be responsible for 为……负责，造成……的原因
be satisfied with 对……满意
be supposed to 应该，被期望……
be sure of 确信
be susceptible to 易受……影响的；易为……左右的
be synonymous with 等同于
be talented at 在……方面有天赋
be tolerable to (intolerable to) 对……可以（不可以）容忍
between... and... 在……与……之间
be unique to 是……独有的，特有的
be willing to 愿意……
be worried about(worry about) 为……忧虑

be worth...ing/noun 值得……
be worthy of...ing/noun 配得上，对得起，当之无愧
burst into 突然开始……
by accident 偶然地
by deadline 截止
by design 故意地，蓄意地
by mistake 错误地
by no means 绝不，无论如何都不……
by order of 奉……的命令
by (in) virtue of 凭借……的力量，由于

C

call off 取消
can (can't) afford to 能（不能）买得起（当使用 to 时，应接动词原形）
can (can't) afford + noun 能（不能）买得起
cannot help... doing 不得不
cannot help but 只能
care for 喜欢……，在意……
catch up with 追上……, 赶上……
catch sight of 看见……
catch someone off guard 使某人措手不及
collaborate with someone in...ing/noun 与……进行合作
commit (time/money/effort) to (a job/... ing) 拨出，调配 (资源、资金等)；承诺……
come into existence 成立，建立
come across 偶然发现，偶然遇到
come down with 染上，得了 (病)
come to terms with 与……达成协议
compensate for 为……做出补偿
conjure up 使……浮现于脑海，想起……
congratulate... on 就……向某人祝贺
consist of (be composed of) 由……组成
consistent with (inconsistent with) 与……一致（不一致）
contact = come in contact with = make contact with 联络……，与……取得联系
contrary to 与……相反
contribute to 促成，捐献
cooperate with 与……合作
cope with 处理，应付

D

deal with 处理，应付
dedicate... to... ing/noun 致力于……
delve into 钻研，深入研究
depend on (upon) (rely on, count on) 依靠……，由……决定
derive from 起源于……
despite 尽管，虽然
devote... to... ing/noun 致力于……
discourage... from 阻止……
differ from (be different from) 与……不同
dispense 分配，分发
dispense with 摒弃，省略，不用
dispossess A of B 剥夺 A 对 B 的权利，从 A 那里夺走 B

E

either A or B 要么 A，要么 B
emerge from 从……中浮现，出现
enable... to 使……能够……
encourage... to 鼓励……
endow A with B 把 B 捐赠给 A
engage in 参与，从事，忙于……
enter into 加入（讨论）；订立（协议）；开始（关系）
excel in (at) 在……方面出色

F

fend off (ward off) 挡开……
fill out 填 写（表格等）……
focus on 致力于，专注于……
for fear of (for fear that) 以免，为了避免……

G

gain(get) an edge over(on) 对……获得优势，胜过……
give a break 休息一下
give way to 给……让路

H

hand in (turn in) 上交，递交
hand out 分布，散发
hands-on 亲身实践的，实际操作的

have an intention of (intend to) 打算……
have a resemblance to 与……相似
have no choice but to 只能……

I

impact on 冲去，对……有影响
in addition to... ing 除了……之外，还……
in an effort to 企图……，努力……
in case of 万一
in charge of 负责……
in contact with 与……保持联络
indulge in 沉溺于……
in favor of 赞成或者支持……
in good/bad shape 处于良好 / 不良的状态
in hand 在手中
in need of 需要
in one's(the) way 阻碍某人
in pursuit of 追求……，寻求……
in recognition of 承认……而……，为酬答……而……
in response to (respond to) 对……做出反应
in regard to 关于……
in search of 寻找……
insist on (insistence on) 坚持，强调……
in spite of 虽然，尽管……, 不顾……
instead of 代替……
instill in 灌输，使获得
insulate against 防止……，与……隔绝
in tandem (with) 与……同时发生
in time 及时
interfere with 妨碍，干扰
intervene in 干涉，介入
in vain 白费地，徒劳地
it is certain that 毫无疑问
it is not until... that 直到……才

J

just as... so 正像……也……

K

keep pace with 并驾齐驱，赶上，跟上
keep up with 跟上……，不落后于……
knock over 偷窃；碰翻；使吃惊；轻易击败

L

leave for 出发去……
liken A to B 把 A 比作 B
limit... to... 使……受……的限制
long for + noun =long to + verb 渴望……
look forward to 期望，盼望
look into 考察，调查，研究
look to 指望，依靠

M

make a living 赚钱生活
make friends (with) 与……交朋友
make room for 给……让出地方
make sense of 搞清……的意思
make sure of (to) 确定，确保

N

neither a nor b　a 和 b 都不
no sooner... than... 一……就……
notify... of 正式将（某事）通知（某人或某团体）
anot only A but also B 不但……而且……
not so much A as B 与其说 A 不如说 B

O

object to noun/...ing 反对，对……反感
of a ……descent 来自于……
offer of 提供（物）；给予（物）；提议
on account of 由于，基于
on display 展出
on foot 步行
on hand 在手边，在附近
only to 不料竟然……，没想到会……
on one’s(the) way 在……的路上
on the brink of 濒于……
on time 按时，准时

P

partake in=take part in=participate in 参与，参加
pass by 从……旁边走过，路过
passion for 对……的激情，爱好
pay for 为……付钱
pay attention to 关注
prefer to 更喜欢……，宁愿……
preoccupy with 全神贯注于……
prey on 捕食，掠夺
prior to 在……之前
protest against 抗议……
put at ease 使……结束，彻底解决……
put away 把……收起，放好
put forth 放出，发表
put off 推迟，拖延
put on hold 搁置，延期
put out 伸出，扑灭，出版

Q

qualify for 有……资格

R

react to 对……做出反应
red-handed 当场抓住，当场逮获
refer to 指……
refrain from 抑制、克制，戒除
regardless of 不管……，不顾……
relate to 涉及，与……有关系
remind... of 提醒……
reply to 回复，回答
respond to 对……做出反应
result in 导致
return to 返回到……
rid A of B 使 A 不能拥有 B
rob A of B 从 A 手里抢走 B

S

save time in 省时间……

search for 搜索，搜寻
see... off 送行，送别
shy of 对……有顾虑；对……畏缩；缺乏
similar to 与……相似
stock-in-trade 存货，现货
stop by 顺便拜访，顺路探望
succeed in 在……中取得成功
succeed to 继承，继任
successor of ……的继承者，继任者
succeed in 在……中获得成功
succeed to 继承，继任
suffer from 受……的折磨，因……而遭受痛苦
suffer through 遭受，挨过
suspect... of (be suspicious of) 怀疑

T

take into account 将……考虑在内
take notice of 注意到……
take the place of 代替，替换
take pride in 以……为骄傲
take place 发生
tend to (have a tendency to) 倾向于……
thanks to (due to, owing to) 幸亏，多亏
the reason (why)... is that ……的原因是……
the same... as 与……同样
to one's heart's content 让……心满意足的是……
to one's surprise 让……吃惊
transfer to 转学到……， 转移到……

U

under (the) control of 在……的控制之下

W

wear out (使) 磨损；(使) 用坏
work in profession 工作
wreak havoc on 肆虐，对……造成巨大的破坏

Z

zoom in/out 放大 / 缩小